They Walk
Among Us

Stephen Shaw

They Walk Among Us

Stephen Shaw's Books

Visit the website: www.i-am-stephen-shaw.com

I Am contains spiritual and mystical teachings from enlightened masters that point the way to love, peace, bliss, freedom and spiritual awakening.

Heart Song takes you on a mystical adventure into creating your reality and manifesting your dreams, and reveals the secrets to attaining a fulfilled and joyful life.

They Walk Among Us is a love story spanning two realities. Explore the mystery of the angels. Discover the secrets of Love Whispering.

The Other Side explores the most fundamental question in each reality. What happens when the physical body dies? Where do you go? Expand your awareness. Journey deep into the Mystery.

Reflections offers mystical words for guidance, meditation and contemplation. Open the book anywhere and unwrap your daily inspiration.

5D is the Fifth Dimension. Discover ethereal doorways hidden in the fabric of space-time. Seek the advanced mystical teachings.

Star Child offers an exciting glimpse into the future on earth. The return of the gods and the advanced mystical teachings. And the ultimate battle of light versus darkness.

The Tribe expounds the joyful creation of new Earth. What happened after the legendary battle of Machu Picchu? What is Christ consciousness? What is Ecstatic Tantra?

The Fractal Key reveals the secrets of the shamans. This handbook for psychonauts discloses the techniques and practices used in psychedelic healing and transcendent journeys.

I am sitting here watching her. She is one of the souls assigned to me. Perched above the driver's cabin I have a great view of the surrounding North Atlantic Ocean. We are sailing away from the coastline of Reykjavik on the hunt for the elusive northern lights or aurora borealis.

Iceland is a fascinating place. We began with the usual guided tour of the Presidential Residence at Bessastaðir; the landmark exhibition building called Perlan (The Pearl); the spectacular Hallgrímskirkja church; and Hafnafjörður, the town where the hidden people or Huldufólk reside (huldu 'pertaining to secrecy' and fólk 'people'). I had to smile at the last location. If only they knew.

A couple of days ago we enjoyed the gorgeous Þingvellir National Park; Gullfoss, the breathtaking two-tiered Golden Waterfall that cascades into a narrow canyon 70 metres deep and 2.5 kilometres long; and the Great Geysir which hurls boiling water up to 70 metres in the air. The highlight was the famous Blue Lagoon, a therapeutic pool of warm and mineral-rich geothermal water carved out of the Svartsengi lava field. I have no idea what it feels like to be immersed in those beautiful waters but she seemed to be blissed out.

Lailah is the one I was ordered to guide and protect. In fact, the brief was 'guide and support'. There are other protégées assigned to me but Lailah holds a special place in my heart. I feel protective. We are cautioned about getting too close to humans. Breaking the rules is hazardous. So I am careful. She has never seen me.

The winter in Iceland is great for exploring the dancing northern lights. This natural phenomenon occurs when electrically charged solar particles enter the earth's atmosphere. Auroras (from the Latin word meaning 'sunrise') are particularly common in the high latitude regions of the Arctic and Antarctic. In northern latitudes the effect is known as the aurora borealis (or the northern lights), named after the Roman goddess of dawn, Aurora, and the Greek word for the north wind, Boreas. In southern latitudes it is called the aurora australis (or the southern lights).

She stands by herself at the bow, one arm hooked firmly over the railing. A quiet one, a bit of a loner, her sparkling intelligence reserved for the few allowed close to her. Lailah is in her early twenties, lithe, flawless pale complexion, dark blonde corkscrew curls sprinkled with scatterings of sunlight, eyes the colour of a summer sky. Why am I drawn to her? We come from different worlds. And I have been alive for a thousand years.

The gasps are audible. The formation seems to come out of nowhere, filling the atmosphere at incredible speed. Tourists gaze in wonderment as the fluorescent green glow illuminates the heavens. I notice the solitary tear rolling down her cheek. The fulfilment of a long held dream – to observe the magnificent aurora borealis!

* * *

On the way back I watch the freezing wind riffling through her hair. Why doesn't she come inside? I am unable to sense temperature or feel things physically but I understand the signs. Besides, I can see the others huddled below deck, enjoying hot chocolate.

It's the whuump! that disrupts my silent world. A freak wave crashes against the boat. People are thrown across the saloon. Lailah! I took my eyes off her for only a second. Where is she? That's her red scarf in the water. No, it can't be. It couldn't have happened. I am torn inside. The Three Immutable Laws. I may not interfere. It is a punishable offence. It will change everything.

I dive into the icy water.

There she is! Struggling in a swirl of darkness, eyes wide with fear. I have to shift my form to save her. I will become visible. She will see me. I reach out, pull her into my energy field, dispel the water and leap back to the boat. No one notices that she was overboard.

The crew scampers among the tourists, offering first aid and calming words of reassurance. Apart from a few scratches and cuts, everyone seems unharmed. The boat sails on uneventfully.

My arm rests gently across her shoulders. It feels so ... right. And so wrong. I have broken the rules and ruined everything. She will be reassigned and I will be never be able to see her again. My heart aches quietly.

"Who are you?" Her eyes gaze up at me, deep pools of longing. I know the incessant questions emblazoned upon her mind. I know her inquisitive energy.

I don't have a name. In your world I am called Michael.

"Why have you been hiding from me all these years?"

There are rules we have to follow.

"Are you an angel?"

You call us angels.

"There are others like you?"

Yes. We are the Guardians.

"I know you. I have felt your presence come and go. No one ever believed me. I begged you to show yourself ... screamed at you ... threw tantrums ... even tried bribery."

You did. I smile kindly at her.

"Are you in trouble now?"

I am.

She grabs me in a tight embrace. "Don't ever leave me."

A sickening anguish courses through my being. What have I done? What unspeakable choice have I made?

The boat docks in the harbour. I shift my energy to become invisible as the tourists disembark. But I stay close to her. Every moment is precious now.

"Show yourself to me," she says imploringly. "Please ..."

When it appears safe I do so.

I have to get to the church in Hallgrímskirkja.

"Why?"

They know. They are expecting me to report.

"How do they know? Are they watching you?"

In my world we are connected to the collective consciousness. Everything is known and shared.

"So you cannot even lie?"

We have free will. The collective consciousness means we operate with transparency, openness and honesty. There is nothing to hide and no need for deceit. There is also no loneliness. We enjoy a natural form of empathy. It's called love.

"Wow. I cannot imagine such a world."

It is wonderful. And these energy bodies can travel anywhere on earth, instantly.

"Why the church?"

Guardians are earth-bound. We tend to congregate in peaceful places. We often gather at religious premises, temples, beaches, oceans, forests, mountains ...

"Are you ever off duty?"

Guardians are connected energetically to their assignments. There is no distance in the energy world. We can be on a beach in Hawaii and hear your call. We can be present with several of our assigned souls at once. We are not limited in the way you are.

"I need to ponder that one."

I must go.

"Please come back. So many questions burn in my mind. This life seems so difficult, such a struggle, so lonely. I can't bear it sometimes. I need you."

I shimmer my energy for her sake. Disappearing instantly seems too harsh.

* * *

There they are, waiting just outside the church. Messengers. The ones allowed to move between the home world and this reality called earth. We step inside and sit on one of the empty grey pews.

You have broken the Three Immutable Laws. The Overseers are displeased.

I nod. What is there to say?

You may not reveal yourself. You may not interfere with free will. You may not interrupt the flow of Life.

I nod again. She would have died. I could not let that happen.

You will be recalled and banned from the earth plane. She will be reassigned. Come with us. We are going home.

A no-win situation. Either way I lose her.

I stand and make as if to follow. But something shifts in me. The others sense it immediately. It's like my consciousness is splitting and I am hovering over a dark chasm. I know what I should do ... yet I am moving away ...

Where are you going?

This time I don't shimmer.

I must find Lailah and repair an impossible situation. She is in the hotel dining room. I sweep across the floor in my usual manner, my long coat flaring behind me. The stares alert me. Attracting to much attention. What is it? The illusory clothes? The walk? Is it the fear in my energy field?

"Michael!" She jumps up and hugs me.

This is terrible. A guide without a plan. A mentor with no idea. I am supposed to have all the answers.

"Are they taking you back?"

I stare at the rose motif in the carpet. *They tried. I'm sorry, I don't know what I am doing.*

She's so young. It's unfair. Everything they warned us about at the academy.

"Will they come after you?"

They will send the Chasers. Messengers with special powers.

She smiles. "I will try to keep up." Her hand moves to cover mine. "I have been aware of you my whole life. Always wished you would appear." A blush tinges her cheeks. "I love you. I cannot explain it."

I am drowning in a deep ocean. Too many rules have been broken. I shouldn't be here. I come from a different reality.

Then it escapes the fetters with a soft sigh.

I love you too.

* * *

Guardians do not sleep. I usually wait until her breathing deepens then disappear to one of the Seychelles islands in the Indian Ocean. Tonight I hold her close and let her rest in my arms. The ceiling becomes a whiteboard to sketch out schemes and solutions.

Blonde curls are scattered across the white pillow. A sleepy eye opens. "You're still here ..." The sweetest smile. Her hand reaches out to touch mine. I wonder if she knows that I cannot physically feel it, only sense the energy.

"Do you have a plan?"

I order orange juice and croissants from room service then gaze across at her. *I have to run. No other choice. And I need to disappear from the knowledge grid.*

"The collective consciousness? How?"

Free will. My mind is like a device hooked to the internet. I cannot hold all the information as it is too much for one entity. I am constantly uploading my experiences to a vast knowledge bank, a bank that all beings can access.

"What happens if you disconnect?"

I lose access to the repository of knowledge and the guidance of the Messengers. I will retain all my own knowledge, learning, experiences and wisdom.

"I'm sorry. Is this my fault?"

I am responsible for my life and my choices.

"Were you aware of my love all these years?"

Yes ... but I steadfastly refused to acknowledge my feelings ... until now.

"Oh."

She is quiet for a few minutes, staring out the window at the snowy mounds.

Then with an earnest expression: "Take me with you. I will go wherever you go."

It's risky. I don't know if I can let you make that choice.

"Have you heard of Joseph Campbell, American mythologist?"

Sure. He ascended to our world in 1987. We shared thoughts a few times. I have to smile. I know what's coming.

"He said: 'Do you want me to tell you something really subversive? Love is everything it's cracked up to be. That's why people are so cynical about it. It really is worth fighting for, being brave for, risking everything for. And the trouble is, if you don't risk anything, you risk even more.'"

Touché.

"Don't judge me by my age. It is our spirit and energy that are pulling each other."

Hey, who is the mentor and guide here?

"I wonder sometimes …" She pokes me and curls into a fit of giggles on the crumpled duvet.

I wait a while, then *You do realise that I do not need to eat or drink or wash or sleep? I am pure energy, existing in a much higher vibrational form than you.*

She yawns in mock insolence. "Say what?"

An inner sigh. Ok, time to risk it all. Let's see what unfolds.

We will leave once you are showered and dressed.

"How will we travel?"

Hold my hand and we jump instantly.

"Seriously?"

Yep. Is there anyone you wish to contact to say your goodbyes?

"You know there is no one. I can walk away from my job. Parents deceased in a car accident when I was five, or so they say. I have no memories prior to ten years old."

Alright.

"Where are we going?"

La Digue Island, Seychelles.

"Why, what's there?"

Nothing.

* * *

We arrive in the late afternoon, her naked toes gently squelching into the pale pink sands of Anse Source d'Argent. The backdrop of towering granite boulders and swaying palms fringes a gorgeous expanse of turquoise water protected from the ocean's waves by a reef. It is one of the most beautiful beaches in the world.

"So this is how you live," she sighs. "Wow ..."

An hour passes. The warm sun dances across her delicate shoulders. A soft breeze teases her curls. Not a word escapes her lips. Silence is my natural state. It is comfortable to sit quietly together.

"Are you going to show me the rest of the island?"

I take her hand. *Do you want to walk or jump?*

"Let's save the jumping for long distances."

Ok.

She seems calm and relaxed. Is she truly unfazed by the sudden revelations or is it a feigned nonchalance? Is this how a young person deals with radical change?

Would you like an overview of La Digue?

"Please."

This is the third largest inhabited island of the Seychelles, with a population of about 2,000 people. It has an area of about 10 square kilometres so most people travel around on bicycles. The temperature during the day varies between 24 and 32 degrees Celsius with occasional heavy rainfall. In the interior is the lovely Veuve Nature Reserve. There are also many guesthouses and hotels, a few restaurants and a dive centre.

"That sounds useful. I will need to find some work."

Yes. Perhaps a hotel where you can shower and eat. At night you can sleep in my energy field, safe and warm and protected.

"Hmm, romantic ..." She beams a radiant smile at me.

We spend a couple of hours wandering along the beaches and eventually settle at the Veuve restaurant, renowned for its traditional Creole cuisine. The menu boasts a wide range of delectable fish dishes and it is not long before she is patting her mouth with the table napkin.

During the next few days Lailah secures a job cleaning hotel rooms. She takes enough shifts to cover her basic needs and we have plenty of time to enjoy the stunning sights. We stroll down to Union Estate Park and watch the giant tortoises, some over 100 years old; climb to Bellevue and savour the spectacular views across the island; and get lost in the Veuve Nature Reserve, chasing for glimpses of the Paradise Flycatcher, a bird with an iridescent blue sheen, blue bill and long black tail streamers.

It is the end of a busy two weeks. We are holding hands and watching the crimson sunset at Anse Coco, an isolated and enchanting beach on the east side of La Digue.

How's the job going?

"I'm not using my psychology degree but it's alright. Every day seems like a wonderful dream ... being here with you ... in this beautiful place."

I put my arm around her and smile.

"What's life about anyway? Sure, I'm young. But this world never made sense to me. Everyone competing for resources when there is an abundance on our planet. A selfish minority who accumulate wealth at the expense of others. Leaders who abuse power and engage in war and genocide. Religious systems that marginalise women and promote disparity and segregation. Governments that fail to provide the fundamental pillars of free health care and free education."

Your world is quite strange.

"I always knew you were there. And that you came from a higher reality." She pauses to trace a spiral in the sand. "How frustrating it must be to watch the human race flounder, to witness the despair, the struggle and the conflict. To not be able to intervene in our affairs."

You have no idea.

"And to watch our painfully slow evolution."

The job requires oodles of patience.

"And then one day you break the rules."

I sigh heavily. *Indeed.*

Silver-tipped waves are unfurling in the mauve light, as if a water-goddess is gently shaking an entrancing magic carpet.

She gazes up at me. "When are you going to deal with the collective consciousness?"

Tomorrow. I will do it tomorrow. I feel apprehensive ... the unknown consequences ...

"May I be with you?"

I would like that.

The moon caresses her soft cheeks while gleaming spotlights slink across the boulders. The soothing swoosh lulls the senses, causing my energy field to expand protectively. Lying on my back, I pull her close and we drift soporifically among the flickering stars.

* * *

Today is a day off from work. I jump Lailah across the island for a shower and breakfast. As long as our energy fields are touching we can travel anywhere together, without physical limitations. She takes it all in her rather cool stride.

Later, picnic basket in hand, we leap to Anse Songe, a small beach on the south coast. We settle in a shaded area and sit facing each other.

"Are you ready?"

Not really. But choices are somewhat limited.

"You know what to do?"

I am consciousness and my intention directs my journey.

"Aha."

See you on the other side.

She smiles lovingly. "I will be right here waiting for you."

Then everything turns black.

"Michael ..."

Engulfed in purple swirls ... lost ... confused ...

"Michael ..."

The agony of aloneness ... such pain ...

"Michael ..."

Must get back to her ... find her light ...

"Michael ..."

I jolt to wakefulness. She is laying on top of me, staring into my eyes.

Lailah. Are you alright? How long was I gone?

"A few hours. Glad you're back."

I put my arms around her and hold her tight.

"How are you feeling?"

It hurts ...

We lay silently embracing on the warm sand.

Is loneliness the human condition?

"It's probably the worst part. The sheer aloneness. The disconnect from everybody and everything. Born alone, die alone. And no matter what you do, you can never fully merge into another being. I think this is what drives us crazy."

Is there anything I can do?

"Chocolate."

Chocolate?

"Yep. Anyway, I am the last person you should be asking for advice. Make some friends. Love someone with all your heart. That might work." She winks at me.

My laughter bursts through the pain.

"Oh yeah, there's that."

What?

"Smile. Laugh. Develop a sense of humour. You are going to need it."

Sounds ominous.

"It's just life ... on the human level."

She grabs a pebble and throws it into the ocean. "Have you still got your superpowers?"

I jump to the nearby islands of Praslin and Mahe; across to Big Ben, the famous bell in the Elizabeth Tower in London; then return to the beach.

Seems so.

"Well, you have more than the rest of us. Not much to complain about."

I guess.

She walks over and gently interlaces her fingers in mine. Our eyes meet. "My dear Michael. We have love, freedom and laughter. I think we are going to be alright."

* * *

The weeks drift by in paradise. We watch the surfers at Grand Anse, lounge in the sun on L'Union Beach, and spend quiet and tender moments at Anse Marron. Every day the swoosh of the ocean massages our spirits and a turquoise vista blesses our eyes. Our evenings are filled with romantic walks amid spectacular pastel-brushed sunsets.

Lailah does not seem to mind the differences between us. Fortunately we have very similar spirits ... able to just sit and be ... hold hands and stare at the waves ... lie in each other's arms and laugh and chat.

"So you cannot feel my touch?" she asks me one afternoon.

This is an energy body not a physical one. I sense your intentions and emotions as energy, as a vibration, as a song.

"As a song?"

Yes. Your thoughts and energy motions are like musical notes. As are mine. For some reason there is a great harmony between our notes. A concord.

"A concord?"

An agreement. A joining. A flow.

"We are making beautiful music together?"

Exactly.

"I love that!"

I smile and squeeze her hand affectionately.

Do you know that the word universe means 'one from many' or 'combined into one'? Every being, every entity, every consciousness is singing its own unique song. The universe is alive with infinite notes and vibrations.

"A cacophony?"

Sometimes. Difficult relationships, romantic dramas, countries at war ... those are discordant notes. However, over time our differences diminish and subside. We are all gradually drifting toward an exquisite concord. It is the destiny of all consciousness. We become One Song.

"I have just fallen deeper in love with you."

Voila!

"Huh?"

Love unites all the notes. Love creates the One Song.

"Kiss me ..."

You know I cannot feel it.

"I don't care."

Slowly and lusciously her lips melt onto mine. Her song becomes serene and upbeat, reminding me of an intricate and beautiful Italian opera. There is no time, only a sweet merging of tender and delicious notes. I am lost in a symphony of passionate love.

Perhaps it is my dazed expression that prompts her question: "You never kissed anyone before?"

It's not part of the job description.

"I was your first kiss?"

Indeed.

"We have some catching up to do ..."

She straddles me and lavishes kisses upon my neck and face. Our mouths meet and start a cosmic dance. Her energy is unfamiliar, seductive and loving, pulling me to a place I have never been. The swooshing ocean ... the azure sky ... the waves of pleasure ... our energies blending ... the inside of me feels like it wants to explode ... rainbow colours ... bright light ... the urge to shout ... to cry out ...

I see your essence! I see you!

"I see you ..."

Swirling into timeless galaxies ... lost in a million suns ... spiralling into a jewelled net of stars. The end of thoughts and words.

We collapse onto the warm sand as the energy slowly subsides.

Hours later, cuddling in the dusky light, I whisper to her sun-kissed curls. *So this is making love. You never mentioned ...*

"You never asked."

You are so beautiful.

"And you."

* * *

It is very dark. A waning moon is barely visible on the horizon. Even the stars seem dimmer. Something is wrong.

Lailah stirs then sits up. "What is it?"

I don't know. Bad feeling.

We scan our surroundings.

"Hey, are there supposed to be dogs on this beach?"

Dogs? Where?

She points. "There, walking toward us from the palm trees."

Flickering red eyes. A curious mix of large wolf and Doberman. I stare back at them, trying to sense their intent.

Chasers!

"Are you sure?"

Never seen one before but I know they are masters at disguising their energy.

"Can you disguise yours?"

I was raised in a world of transparency and openness. I don't know how.

"Can you try?"

They have already seen us. It's too late.

"What are you going to do?" Her song is spiked with fear.

Stop talking. Let me think.

The three Chasers take up positions on our flanks and by the boulders, leaving the crashing waves behind us. The vibrations around and behind them are distorting the energy matrix, making it difficult for me to jump. A menacing tone: *You have transgressed the Immutable Laws. We can take you home by force.*

A deathly still pervades. Nobody moves.

Suddenly Lailah's voice erupts in a high-pitched scream: "How dare you contravene our free will! You think you are immune to your own laws?"

Lailah! What are you doing? Let me handle this.

She hurtles past the nearest Chaser, her arms flailing. "I won't let you take him! I won't let you!"

Within seconds she is pounced upon.

Distraction in progress, I grab the real Lailah and run toward the water. We get clear of the distortion and surge deep into the ocean.

Here we wait in the darkness. Not moving, not talking. I emanate just enough light so she can see me.

Hours later we jump to the Maldives, another island nation just east of the Seychelles and south-west of India. Rangali and Rangalifinolhu are two private islands joined by a 500-metre footbridge built over gorgeous blue waters. A perfect place for our next hideaway.

* * *

Considering my ability to read energy fields and the extensive knowledge I have accumulated over a thousand years, I offer my services as a counsellor in the resort. I am disconnected from the energy grid so can work unnoticed and it's an opportunity to help people. Besides, what's another broken rule?

The owner is soon impressed enough to let us use a small beach villa. Lailah finds work at the over-water Spa Retreat adjoining our island; an easy commute along a wooden pier.

We use our free time to explore the magnificent surroundings. Rangali Island contains 79 contemporary beach villas nestled among tropical greenery while the smaller Rangalifinolhu Island, linked by a footbridge and ferry system, offers 50 romantic water villas. Tourists can enjoy the usual water sports and excursions, including snorkelling and diving. The tropical paradise is encompassed by a lagoon, coral reef, glorious white sandy beaches and breathtaking ocean views.

We are walking hand in hand along the magnificent shoreline.

"I love it here. I'm never going back to my old life."

Understandable.

"Do you believe in spiritual gravity?"

Meaning?

"You know, the gradual drawing of one's spirit to certain realities. The inevitable movement toward the finest and most accurate expression of oneself."

Elucidation required.

"Well, you and I feel most at home on these tropical beaches … and with each other … and we both prefer work that serves humanity. There is a natural drawing … a pull … causing us to gravitate toward certain places and people."

True …

"So it is inevitable that we would find each other … and that our life would play out in this fashion."

Are you saying we have no choice?

"I think there is a script inside each one of us ... resulting from innate traits and dispositions and collated experience ... that influences and guides our choices."

Hmm ...

"If the Messengers were surveying your mind, they should have known you would run."

They know everything. Our lives are completely open.

"Then why are those beings chasing you?"

I stare at the ruffling waves. Words have deserted me. A White Tern suddenly descends from the skies and starts harassing us. We back away rapidly. Perhaps we have disturbed a nest.

"A timely cosmic distraction."

I look at her quizzically.

She sighs. "Maybe we are not supposed to be asking those questions."

Ha! You? Your mind burns with curiosity.

"Don't you wonder about everything?" She bends down and scoops a handful of sand then flings it high in the air. "I want to know the answers. I want to understand the reasons. Why? Why? Why?"

Let's go for a swim.

Clothes are strewn on the beach as we race to the water ... we plunge into the translucent waves ... our toes curling on the ocean floor ... exhilarating shouts as we splash each other furiously ... heading out into the deep to discard our frustration and confusion ...

Exhausted, we return to the shallows ... tumbling into each other's arms ... giggling ... kissing ... Then we stand for a long while and gaze out across the rippling surf.

"I have never seen so many shades of blue."

It is incredibly beautiful.

"What now?"

Early dinner at the all-glass undersea Ithaa Restaurant. I booked a table for 6pm. There needs to be plenty of daylight to fully capture the experience.

"Did you say 'undersea'?"

Yes. The ceiling and walls are made of glass. The restaurant is 5 metres underwater.

"Wow." A brief pause. "You don't eat or drink."

No worries. I created an energy illusion to escape the Chasers. I am sure I can fake this.

She hooks her arm into mine. "What are we waiting for? Take me to dinner."

Judging by the smiles, the Ithaa Restaurant is a gastronomist's dream, and the panoramic views of the reef and marine life are fabulous. Lailah looks so content that I determine to make a booking for the alfresco Japanese Koko Grill Restaurant later in the week.

We fall asleep on the porch of our villa, watching the stars. Everything is good in our world.

* * *

I place the steaming coffee on the outside table. Sure enough, the aroma rouses her.

Hey, sleepyhead.

"Hey ..."

She shuffles on the deck chair, shifting into a more comfortable position. "Had the strangest dream."

You did?

"Yeah." She rubs her eyes. "One of those vivid dreams. You were in it ... standing with your back against an immense iridescent crystal ... in a green-tinged world. Very peaceful ... yellow sparks appearing and receding everywhere. And this huge building with pillars ... radiating a powerful white energy ... it was seeping through the windows and under the doors. I could hear a voice refusing me entry."

Sounds like my world.

"Really?"

Yep. Would you like some breakfast?

"No. Tell me ..."

The crystal symbolises the repository of knowledge. Every being constantly uploads experiences and learning into the knowledge bank. Any being can download information at will. It's as simple as typing a question into an internet search engine.

"So the answers are only as good as the information stored in the crystal."

True.

"Who administers the knowledge bank?"

That is the job of the seven Overseers. They monitor everyone and everything and enforce the rules.

"Are they transferring all their experiences into the crystal?"

Of course.

"How do you know?"

Our world values transparency and openness.

"How do you know?"

Uh …

"On earth, no internet search engine will deliver classified material. It doesn't matter how you phrase the question. If information is not uploaded, then it is not available."

What are you saying?

"It seems that the rules on your world don't apply to everyone. Look at the Chasers. They are allowed to break the Three Immutable Laws."

Words have abandoned me again. I stumble along my conflicting thoughts.

"I'm sorry. I am just asking questions. Maybe there is something you are missing."

Do you mind if I go for a walk? I need to contemplate this.

She gives me a hug. "I will be right here."

I jump across to Rangalifinolhu Island and sit on the north beach. Perhaps the serene undulations will swoosh some sense into me. I have no idea what's going on. In all these years I have simply followed orders, kept within the boundaries and taken good care of my charges.

I am a Messenger who chose to become a Guardian. While Messengers can move freely between my world and earth reality, Guardians are earth-bound for the duration of their assignments. I consider this a minor sacrifice; the fulfilment of mentoring human souls far outweighs the loss of my home. I have been a Guardian for the last 300 years and it has brought me great joy.

Until recently I was always connected to the collective consciousness. This meant that no matter where I was located, I never felt alone. And the knowledge bank provided access to the vast knowledge and experience of my fellow beings.

I don't pretend to have all the answers. All I know is that my world is beautiful and peaceful. There is no competition and no conflict. There is no dishonesty or selfishness. Everyone is working toward the good of all beings. Everything is shared openly and privacy is redundant.

And yet ... some rules are clearly not followed. Is it a rogue element? Are there beings who have a private agenda? Is there a higher purpose?

The problem is I don't know what I don't know.

I stare at the glassy turquoise water for another hour then jump back to Lailah. She is still lounging on the deck chair, accompanied by a breakfast tray and orange juice.

"Anything clearer?" she asks between mouthfuls.

Not at all. Just have to accept my knowledge limitations for now.

"It will come to you."

You not working today?

"No. Will you explain more of my dream, please?"

Hmm ... the yellow sparks are energy beings coming and going ... the huge building is the Sacred Temple where the Keepers of the Light reside. No one may enter this temple. The Keepers are informally known as the 'burning ones' because such a bright light emanates from them that no one, not even other angelic beings, can look upon them.

"You used the word 'angelic'."

I shrug. *It's a term familiar to humans.*

"Feels ... nice."

Unfortunately, myths abound. We don't have wings. We are pure energy. This is what I really look like.

"A white-yellow basketball with energy sparks?"

Yep. Or this.

"A gently floating white-yellow mist?"

I am translating into your reality as best I can.

"Wow, Michael." Tears are trickling down her cheeks. "You are so beautiful."

This is probably not the best time to remind her that angels have no names. That's another human ascription. We recognise each other by our energy signatures. Our essences are what distinguish us.

I put my arm around her. *I love you, my precious person.*

A few tissues later, "I love you too."

We hold each other awhile, then "Let's go snorkelling over the reefs today."

Ok.

"Just one question: Has any being ever looked upon the burning ones?"

As far as I know, never. Except for that darn hummingbird!

"What hummingbird?"

A luminous hummingbird with green, silver and gold plumage. I watched it fly out the temple window.

"It had been inside the temple?"

Indeed.

"Imagine that!"

We stroll to the jetty and climb aboard a traditional Turkish yacht. The tourists are out for a snorkelling and dolphin-spotting excursion so it should be fun. To blend in we follow the procedures, but once in the water I draw Lailah into my energy field. Without the need for surface oxygen we are able to explore the depths with impunity.

We hover beneath enormous white-bellied manta rays, swim on the back of a speckled whale shark, and frolic with a pod of smiling dolphins. Then we cruise along the reef, enjoying the darting and swaying marine life.

By the end of the afternoon Lailah is tired and exhilarated. "Thank you so much. Together we seem to have the best of both worlds."

With that insightful comment resonating in our spirits, we sail back to the island and settle down to a relaxing evening. Considering her predilection for healthy foods, dinner will no doubt be a light and tasty pasta salad. Hopefully we will fall asleep under the stars again.

* * *

"Let me see if I understand the levels," she says upon waking.

Does your mind ever switch off?

"Not really."

She cuddles close into my arms, her head on my chest.

"You've got the Keepers of the Light who no one ever sees. Presumably they are super-knowledgeable and mega-wise. They are inputting an overview and strategic guidance into the knowledge bank, based on their contact with the Light. This is then translated into details and specifics by the Overseers who are essentially administrators and enforcers."

As far as I understand, that is correct.

"So the first issue we need to consider is: Was anything lost in translation?"

Ok ...

"The Overseers have endowed certain Messengers with special powers and given them permission to break the Laws. These beings are called Chasers. Their job is to rein in and halt errant behaviour. Chasers and Messengers can operate in both realities."

Correct again.

"Then there are the Guardians who, I surmise, have hearts of gold and infinite patience."

I smile.

"The second issue is: Do the Overseers make all the knowledge available or do they deem certain information above your grade?"

Something to ponder.

"What exactly is the function of the Messengers?"

They mostly operate in my world as teachers and guides. Sometimes they come to earth to inspire a movement, encourage a paradigm shift or soothe during a crisis. They greet and mentor ascended human souls too.

"You mean humans who pass away on earth?"

Yes. Some souls transition to our world because they are ready for that level of connection, peace and love.

"Not all souls?"

Of course not. You are consciousness and your intention directs your journey.

"Meaning?"

Remember your idea of spiritual gravity?

"Uh huh."

Your soul essence is drawn to certain realities. It depends on what you wish to experience and learn. Certain souls would be repelled by my world. Others would immediately call it home.

"Some people would shun living in heaven with the angels?"

Careful about propagating that myth. Many people on your earth would be very happy to rest in my world. And it may feel like heaven. But not everyone yearns for knowledge and peace. Some crave adventure and drama. Every soul is at a different evolutionary point.

"Oh, I see."

There are infinite realities and some souls aspire to explore other dimensions.

"Are some realities closer to the Source?"

Now you are on the right track. There are many realities on the way to the Source. You choose your own journey. It all depends on what you seek, what you desire.

"Your world is very close to the Source, isn't it?"

Yes, Lailah, it is.

"It kinda begs the question."

It does?

"Yes. What are we doing here in the first place?"

My world is populated with interesting souls. A man called Shamseddin Hafiz ascended in 1390. Once, while discussing earth, he said to me 'There is only one reason we have followed God into this world: to encourage laughter, freedom, dance and love.'

"The things you say make my heart beat faster." She grabs my hand and looks up at me. "For me, heaven is being with you."

I kiss her on the forehead. *I feel the same.*

She glances at the clock and scrambles out of bed. A flurry of clothes and swift brushing of hair. "I am going to be late for work. Please jump me."

I deliver her to the Spa Retreat then wander back along the beach. A bright sun is sparkling upon light blue waters. Waves are unfurling across the reef. The shimmering horizon entrances me. It is going to be another glorious day.

* * *

A month has gone by. Finally a chance to settle and establish a routine. I may be able to live anywhere but I think Lailah needs a bit of stability.

It is easy living in paradise. Every human enjoys breathing fresh air ... basking in radiant warmth ... feasting on tropical fruits and healthy salads ... luxuriating amid calm ocean swoosh ... swimming in refreshing waters ... walking along dazzling beaches ... holding hands and watching mesmerising sunsets. She says she has never been happier.

As for me, I miss being plugged into the knowledge bank. I yearn for that feeling of belonging, of universal connection, of instant and open communication. But I have gained an intimate friend and lover. There is something wonderful about discarding the layers and secrets, and getting to know another's heart. At times she stares at me with such intense love, it feels as if we are melting into each other.

I promised to take her to the Koko Grill Restaurant and tonight's the night. Once my last appointment is finished, I stroll down to the Japanese Water Garden.

There she is, walking along the beach in a flowing white sarong. A full moon is rising and splashing the sand in gleaming silver. What a wonderful sight! Perhaps I have a lover's bias ... but don't all lovers view through the heart?

Hey you ...

"Hey ..."

Our hands interlace. She looks so beautiful.

Let's find our table.

The hostess welcomes us. Our nine-course Japanese dinner commences. The open-air restaurant nestles beneath a blanket of twinkling stars. Turquoise waves are softly lapping the shore. A gentle breeze caresses our naked feet.

We chat about our work for a while then disappear into fits of laughter for no good reason. Maybe Hafiz was right after all ...

As the sixth course is served I notice a ripple in the energy field. I scan the environment quietly; no need to alarm Lailah. A waiter is standing two metres away. Perhaps he is an observing apprentice. He looks innocuous.

"What's with his eyes?"

Excuse me?

"His eyes ..."

Ah, so they do have a giveaway. A red glimmer. There are more flickers in the trees. They have found us again.

Act natural. Stroke my leg and smile. Then stand up and walk to the washroom. Don't look back and don't run.

I begin talking to the chef in Japanese. Soon we are sharing amusing cookery stories and clinking shot glasses of sake. The Chasers are teaching me about my own capabilities. With the chef obscuring the view I create an illusory copy of myself, a copy that makes a sudden mad dash for the ocean. No doubt they remember our previous escape.

A terrible noise ensues. The waiters must think a wild animal is loose. Trees rustle, clouds of sand kick up, then a huge collision in the water.

I slip away soundlessly and find Lailah. She is shivering in the washroom. "I'm scared," she whispers. "How did they find us?"

Shh ...

This time I will put some distance between us. I cloak our energy and jump high in the sky, passing east over Malaysia, Indonesia, Papua New Guinea and the northern tip of Australia. We land on one of the magical islands that make up French Polynesia in the South Pacific Ocean.

Bora Bora, also known as The Romantic Island, is just 29 kilometres long and lies in a protected lagoon edged by white sandy shores and plentiful coconut trees. In the centre of the island are the remnants of an extinct volcano. The time difference means we have arrived in the early morning.

I sigh a little. *We start again.*

"You sure love your beaches."

Guardians have no physical sense of touch but our visual apparatus is acutely sensitive. Also the energies near oceans are particularly agreeable.

"This place has an unusual layout."

Indeed. Bora Bora is the centrepiece with most of the hotels located on the surrounding islets: Motu Tapu, Motu Ahuna, Tevairoa, Motu Tane, Motu Mute, Motu Tufari, Motu Pitiaau, Sofitel Motu, Motu Toopua and Toopuaiti.

"Shall we take a tour? A little island hopping perhaps?" She winks at me.

I slip her arm into mine and off we go. For the next two hours there is a cascade of "spectacular!" and "breathtaking!" and "wow!"

Coconut?

She nods. "Mmm, please … the juice is delicious and nutritious."

I crack open the shell and pass it to her. After she has quaffed the liquid I break the coconut into pieces. She munches happily.

We finally settle on Motu Toopua. Her body clock says it is night-time so I cradle her in my energy field. It is not long before she is asleep.

* * *

"What are we going to do about the Chasers?" she asks, waking and stretching in the afternoon sun.

Keep running I guess. This is a lifestyle for which I am totally unprepared.

"How do you think they found us?"

They seem to be like sniffer dogs tracking our energy. I have never been on the receiving end of Chasers. I don't know how they operate.

"Do you think they intend to harm us?"

My world is predominantly peaceful so I doubt it. However, they can use force to bring me in. I squeeze her hand. *We'll be ok. I will protect you and keep you safe.*

"It's not me I'm worried about."

What do you mean?

"You said I will be reassigned if they catch us. I speculate that my life will continue as usual on earth. But what will happen to you? Do you even know?"

Banned from your reality. Unable to travel here. Other than that, no idea.

"I don't trust those in power anymore. There are too many anomalies. The rules should apply to everyone."

Indeed.

"Why can't we live in peace? What harm is our love doing anyone?"

I bury my toes in the sand and stare at the exquisite shades of blue.

You want to go pearl-diving? You get to keep what we find.

"Sounds brilliant!"

We will search for natural ones – they're quite rare.

"What other types are there?"

Pearls are either cultured or natural. A pearl is formed when an irritant lands within the soft tissue of a living shelled mollusc; in order to protect itself the mollusc deposits layers of nacre over the irritant, which forms a pearl over time. Cultured or farmed pearls are created when a human intervenes and places an irritant in the mollusc. The majority of pearls sold around the world are cultured.

"So the natural ones must be very valuable."

Yes, but in the wild you may have to open hundreds of oysters to find one pearl. This is harmful and unethical so the cultured ones are a preferred choice. During our dive I will scan the energies to ensure we only collect pearl-bearing oysters.

"Is there a value-guide? Are there different colours?"

Natural pearls are very rare and the most valuable. The ideal pearl is perfectly round and smooth.

Of the cultured pearls the most valuable are South Sea pearls, grown in the elusive Pinctada maxima (gold-lip and silver-lip pearl oyster) primarily in Australia, the Philippines and Indonesia. They come in hues of white, cream, pink, silver and gold.

This is followed by Tahitian pearls, often referred to as black pearls, grown in the Pinctada margaritifera (black-lip pearl oyster) right here in French Polynesia. Black pearls are seldom black; they are usually shades of green, purple, aubergine, grey, silver, blue or peacock.

Next are Akoya pearls, grown in a hybridisation of the Pinctada fucata martensii and Pinctada fucata chemnitzii (akoya pearl oyster) in Japan, China, South Korea, Vietnam and Australia. Colours produced include pink, silver, white, cream, gold, blue, grey and black.

Least valuable of the cultured pearls are freshwater pearls, usually grown in freshwater mussels.

"Good to know."

I suddenly realise why she is asking all these questions. Lailah never complains about anything, but being continually uprooted and leaving everything behind must be distressing. If we collect enough pearls for a necklace, it will be the one thing she always takes with her.

Can you survive on coconut for now? You don't want to dive on a heavy stomach.

"Sure."

While she is eating I draw a map of the territories in the sand.

French Polynesia, commonly known as Tahiti, consists of five main island groups called archipelagos: the Society Islands, the Tuamotu Islands, the Marquesas Islands, the Gambier Islands and the Austral Islands. Bora Bora is one of the Society Islands. Our best chance of finding pearls will be around the Tuamotu-Gambier archipelagos.

"You're in charge."

We'll start with the Tuamotu Islands. First stop: the waters of Manihi, Island of Pearls.

"Are you going to put me in a protective bubble again?"

Of course. You ready?

We make the jump then head deep into the dark blue ocean. Lailah manages to transition quickly from wide-eyed to calm and relaxed. It is so serene down here. Coy stingray hover as we move underwater along the islands. It takes about an hour to locate five pearl-bearing oysters.

Another leap and we arrive at Mangareva, one of the Gambier Islands. We dive again. Scanning the energy fields brings great rewards: seven more oysters! She looks delighted.

Back on solid ground. It's twilight. *Have you got money or anything to trade? You are going to be hungry soon. We can open these oysters later.*

"Are you crazy? I can't wait until after dinner! Let's do it now."

I prise an oyster very slowly.

She punches me in the arm. "Come on! Stop teasing me."

A few minutes later they are laid out on a white shirt. We are very fortunate. Nine perfectly round and three irregular-shaped Tahitian pearls. A mix of gorgeous colours that harmonise perfectly.

I have an idea. Select your least favourite irregular pearl.

"This one."

We are on Mangareva, largest island in the region and hub of the pearl industry. Let's find someone to string these for you. We'll offer that pearl.

Any natural pearl creates excitement. Soon we have secured accommodation, dinner and enough cash to last a month. The trader gets a good deal. Two days later we pick up the necklace. I scrutinise the energy fields – yep, same nine pearls. Lailah is over the moon. And, although undoubtedly the last thing on her mind, she is now very wealthy.

We head back to Bora Bora. Neither of us needs to work for a while. Fortunately we enjoy each other's company and have become experts at doing nothing. It's the idyllic life of love, freedom, laughter and dance. What more is required?

* * *

Island living is not for the faint-hearted. Every day we gaze across magnificent turquoise and cobalt waters gleaming in the expansive sunlight. The air temperature and water temperature average about 26 degrees Celsius all year round, and occasional rain nurtures the lush tropical slopes and keeps the valleys blossoming with hibiscus. When we are not lazing in the shade or splashing along the reef, we meander along one of the many beaches. We lie in each other's arms and watch pink-and-gold sunsets and count the minutes until a glowing moon appears.

"Can you see yourself living like this forever?" she asks one morning.

In paradise? With my heart overflowing?

"Good point."

Are you bored?

"A little. People everywhere dream about this kind of life. No work. Sunshine, oceans, palm trees. And it is amazing."

Yes, and ...

"I don't know. I just question life, that's all."

Meaning?

"Why do people work so hard? What's the point? You chase an education or skill set, then a romantic relationship, then a mortgage, then children, then start the cycle again with their school and college. And you land up working all hours just to maintain a lifestyle."

It's one choice.

"And our societies attempt to bend our will and manipulate our desires through relentless advertising, media propaganda, politico-economic coercion and religious ideology. Most religious people have never seen an angel."

You need to quit calling me an angel. I am an advanced being from a reality close to the Source.

"It may just be a term but you are the angels we have spoken about for centuries. Is it not you beings who are mentioned in countless religious stories?"

I cough softly and brush the sand with my foot. *Beings from various dimensions have visited earth.*

"What kind of beings?"

They have different names. Humans called them gods.

"Where are they now?"

Their presence fostered dependence and created disempowered peoples. Supplication began to replace autonomy, strategy and hard work. So they spread their advanced teachings and left the earth. Their legacy is now lost in the myths of history.

"And the angels?"

We have been quietly watching over you. Our intervention in human affairs is limited by the Three Immutable Laws.

"Remind me again."

You may not reveal yourself. You may not interfere with free will. You may not interrupt the flow of Life.

"How long have the laws been in existence?"

From time immemorial.

"So you stand by and watch a world destroying itself. Pollution, war, genocide, poverty, disease, suffering, struggle. It's driving us crazy!"

The idea is that humans learn to act responsibly. That they learn to love each other and their planet. Treat each other with respect, equality and kindness. Work together to promote true democracy, egalitarian economics and impeccable values. Irrespective of gods and angels that may or may not exist.

"Hello! It ain't working."

This beautiful woman seems to put a wobble in my thinking. Everything was peaceful until I revealed myself to her. I did my job, followed the rules and trusted the Overseers. Doubt is now weaving its way through my tapestry of faith.

What am I supposed to do?

"I don't know, but something has to change."

Seems that way.

"I feel torn. Not everyone has these choices. I am playing on a sun-kissed beach while others slave away under oppressive systems. It is no different to you being ensconced in your serene energy world while watching the earth burn. But I also love my life and don't want it to change. All I ever wanted was to be with you and … just be."

I understand.

"Thank you for listening."

Perhaps there is a greater plan. I just can't see it yet.

She shrugs. "Perhaps."

What do you want to do today? You said you're a little bored.

"Only a little. We have a good life."

Why don't we take a cruise on a catamaran? We can afford it.

"That's a great idea!"

Come on. Let's jump to the booking office.

Soon the wind is tousling her golden hair. The boats cuts across undulating waves, delivering the tourists to a number of stunning locations. The visual feast culminates in a rose sunset that illuminates a never-ending horizon.

Over the next few weeks I organise a number of activities to balance our 'nothing time'. A 4x4 excursion along the overgrown forest roads that wind high above the lagoon, with pauses to absorb the awesome panoramic views; guided hikes to Mount Pahia and Mount Otemanu; an exploration of the ancient Marae temples along the coast; horse riding along the beach; and a fun evening at a sand-floor restaurant proffering delicious charbroiled seafood.

Lailah visits a Polynesian spa and gets pampered with an invigorating massage, a body wrap in banana tree leaves, and a herbal rain shower. We spend time relaxing on the gorgeous Matira beach and take long swims in the azure lagoon.

We are lying on our backs under a starry sky. The moon is throwing streaks of greyish white across the sand and dark wavelets are gently rippling in the background.

"Three months. Has to be a record for us."

Was thinking the same.

"I was wondering if we should do a pre-emptive jump ... before they find us."

Any locations in mind?

"I have nine Tahitian pearls on my necklace. Maybe we could collect a few from the South Sea."

That would be Australia, mate!

"If we leave now I can take all my clothes too."

Hmm ... crossing the International Date Line means we would land tomorrow afternoon.

"That's so weird."

Suits me. We get to see another sunset.

"Let's do it!"

Although I can translocate instantly, I prefer to leap more slowly with Lailah so she has the opportunity to enjoy the scenery. As we move through the air with her backpack, I glance down at the luminous sands last time. Red flickers on the beach. Talk about timing.

* * *

It is mid-afternoon on Fraser Island, located off the east coast of Queensland, Australia. The gradual landing affords a spectacular view of the rainforests with 1,000-year-old trees. This World Heritage Site, also the world's largest sand island, comprises 1,840 square kilometres of unspoiled natural paradise.

"May I say 'wow' again?"

Absolutely.

"Wow!"

She is utterly enraptured. "You seem to know the best islands on the planet."

I know a few.

"Where are we going to settle?"

Kingfisher Bay Resort, recipient of numerous environmental, tourism and architectural awards. It will provide a secure base and a place to unpack your clothes. We can't always sleep under the stars.

"Sounds perfect. Do we need to sell another of the irregular-shaped pearls?"

Yes. I'll take care of it.

"I would like to find a way to serve humanity again. Perhaps through a community foundation or charitable trust."

That's a great idea.

Fraser Island is a magical place. The ensuing weeks provide the opportunity to explore the diverse landscape, from the surf-pounded beaches and huge sculpted sand dunes to the luxuriant rainforests and numerous crystal clear freshwater lakes.

After much investigation we find a suitable charitable trust in Queensland and begin to offer our time and services. We intersperse our charity work with rambles through the Great Sandy Conservation Park, situated on the mainland just south of the island. The northern part of the park adjoins Rainbow Beach which edges into the Coral Sea – places as beautiful as their names suggest.

One morning we join a tourist excursion to the calm waters of Hervey Bay which provide shelter for humpback whales and their calves during their migration to Antarctica. The boat delivers us into an arena of acrobatic frolicking with magnificent displays of breaching, tail flapping and pectoral slapping. It is a wonderful and breathtaking sight.

On the way back I notice Lailah staring thoughtfully at the waves.

Where are you, sweetheart?

"Hmm? Oh, I was just dreaming about South Sea pearls."

Ah yes. One of the reasons we came to live here.

"I absolutely adore my necklace and it would be lovely to extend it beyond these iridescent nine. Also, we could sell a few to fund our lifestyle and contribute more to humanitarian causes."

That is good to hear.

A sigh escapes my lips.

"Something bothering you?"

Wouldn't it be great if every wealthy person began to fund humanitarian and save-the-planet projects? There are abundant resources on this planet, more than enough for everyone. They just need to be shared.

"Yep. And many governments spend ten to fifty times more on their military than they do on education. It's absurd."

These days corporations run most Western countries with governments merely acting as puppets to the CEOs. We need the individuals at the top to make sensible decisions. Shareholders and wealthy individuals should be investing their excess profits in renewable energy, genetic medicine and upgraded education systems, with the aim of uplifting the entire planet.

"You mean energy that comes from resources which are continually replenished, like geothermal heat, sunlight, wind, rain, waves and tides?"

For starters. Or maybe they could release and develop the free-energy patents of Nikola Tesla. Why keep these hidden any longer? Do the oil companies need to be any richer?

"What is genetic medicine?"

It studies the role of genes and proteins identified in the Genome Project and attempts to understand the functional consequences of pathogenic genetic variants. Ultimately the research knowledge is translated into healthcare benefits including person-specific diagnosis, management and treatment.

"And the education issue?"

First of all, education should be free. It is a fundamental right and one of the sacred pillars underpinning all societies. Secondly, school education is too long and often contains outdated or useless subjects. Pupils and their mentors need a diverse and life-relevant selection of subjects. Earlier specialisation should be allowed and there needs to be greater use of technology. Elite schools and top professors need to create online teaching facilities to reach a global audience. Class entrance should be based on interest and ability not age.

"No doubt that is just the tip of the iceberg."

Indeed. The real issue is this planet's approach to wealth.

"What do you mean?"

The promise of capitalism and trickle-down economics.

"I'm listening."

Capitalism promised to elevate everyone to a much higher standard of living. Trickle-down economics meant that the financial success of the 1% (the connected and privileged elite getting richer every day) would flow down and automatically benefit the 99% (the ordinary people struggling to get by).

During the 1980s, Reagan and Thatcher began the destruction of unions and cleared the way for the implementation of free-market principles. The emergence of globalisation ensured that almost every corner of the planet became inextricably connected. Over the next 30 years we watched the destabilisation of national economies and the impoverishment of people around the world, culminating in the great global recession of 2008. Entire countries are now debt slaves and joblessness is rife.

There is no trickling down, instead there is a hoovering up. The 1% keep getting wealthier, the middle class is shrinking, and the poor are being devastated.

"Devastated?"

Almost a billion people on this planet do not have access to clean drinking water. Almost 3 billion do not have access to adequate sanitation. Consequently around 700,000 children die every year from diarrhoea. That's almost 2,000 children a day. How many of the 1% notice this? How many care?

"That's shocking!"

Karl Marx ascended to our world in 1883. He predicted that the capitalist system would ultimately impoverish the masses as the world's wealth became concentrated in the hands of a greedy few, resulting in economic crises and heightened conflict between the rich and working classes. He said 'Accumulation of wealth at one pole is at the same time accumulation of misery, agony of toil, slavery, ignorance, brutality, mental degradation, at the opposite pole'.

"The failure of capitalism."

I am not sure if capitalism is the problem. People want to be rewarded directly and fairly for their efforts. Capitalism fosters entrepreneurship and demands high levels of innovation, quality and service. What we need is responsible not laissez-faire capitalism. Governments need to regulate and protect the economy. Power needs to revert to the workers.

People need to reclaim political and economic democracy. What are they waiting for? When will they finally rise up?

Lailah is staring at me with wide eyes. "I guess when there is enough suffering."

I sigh again. *Indeed. Now let's plan our expedition.*

"Where are we going?"

North along the coast: Lady Elliot Island, Great Keppel Island, Hamilton Island, including a tour of the Great Barrier Reef.

"Sounds exciting."

Ok to leave in the morning?

"Oh yes!"

She is beaming a big smile. Her happiness tickles my heart.

* * *

And so begins our adventure along coral gardens, turquoise waters and sun-drenched beaches. The islands average a year-round temperature of 27 degrees Celsius, making it very pleasant for Lailah. We hike the interior winding trails and relish the acres of bush land and abundant wildlife.

The highlight is the magnificent Great Barrier Reef, the world's largest coral reef system, composed of over 2,900 individual reefs and 900 islands stretching over 2,600 kilometres. Together we dive the warm clear waters and encounter an array of whales, dolphins, porpoises, dugongs and sea snakes, as well as numerous clownfish, red bass, red-throat emperor, snapper and coral trout. It is a serene and vibrant paradise!

Repeated underwater excursions reveal drifting turtles, sharks, stingray, skates and chimaera. The cutest seahorses float by, evading our attempts to touch them. My protective energy field means there are no physical limits for Lailah, allowing us to scour the depths for the elusive giant clams.

Eventually we surface the sapphire waters and leap onto Hamilton Island, strewing twenty-five clams along the beach. It takes about half an hour to prise them all. Then we sit and admire the gleaming collection of white, cream, pink, silver and gold South Sea pearls.

These will complete your necklace.

"And help a lot of people."

I gaze fondly at her. Is it possible to fall ever deeper in love?

We make the jump back to Fraser Island and collect Lailah's backpack from reception. A good night's sleep followed by a couple of days running errands and we are ready to recommence our work with the charitable trust. It feels good to be serving humanity again.

At the end of the week I collect the restrung pearls. She now has eighteen in total, artistically arranged so that each colour counterpoints the adjacent one. I pick a few pinkish-cream flowers and scatter the petals over the duvet, then lay her dream necklace on a soft cloth. When she arrives home and makes the discovery, there is an ecstatic shriek. She gives me a big hug and a tearful "Thank you so much."

The routine is good for Lailah. The two-bedroom villa at Kingfisher Bay Resort has its own kitchen and laundry, so we don't have to patronise expensive restaurants. Our weekdays are filled with humanitarian work and our weekends reserved for eco-tours, walks along Seventy-Five Mile beach, jaunts to the Champagne Pools and excursions into the rainforests.

There is not much more you can ask from life. We are great companions; we do what we love; and we are surrounded by exquisite natural beauty. Time blurs happily.

One afternoon we join a tourist mini-bus to view Pile Valley's lush Satinay and Brush Box forests. This affords us the pleasure of some company and offers Lailah the opportunity to enjoy a conversation with someone other than me. As long as I keep a low profile and don't answer too many questions, everything remains secure.

We are sitting in the back. I am staring out the window amid the constant chit-chat. Hmm ... Was that a red flicker in the tree? I move quickly to get another look. The vehicle swerves, causing me to avert my gaze. "Sorry guys, something in the road." The driver glances at me in the mirror.

I give Lailah's leg a nonchalant squeeze. It's our signal. Be cool, act normal, give nothing away. She continues her friendly banter for a few minutes, then points toward the forest and screams in mock horror "It's alive!" Heads turn. We jump instantly. It's not the way I prefer to leave. And it's probably going to create an urban myth.

* * *

The Chasers are clearly relentless, devious and cunning. They are not going to give up and this is not the way we want to live ... on the edge and on the run.

We have landed in Langkawi, Malaysia, an archipelago of 104 islands in the Andaman Sea, just off the mainland coast of north-western Malaysia.

"Another group of islands."

Yep. And at high tide the official island count reduces to 99.

"Note to self."

You sound despondent.

"We left a good life ... and my backpack."

Sorry. I feel frustrated too.

"I don't care about property and possessions. I do care about our love and our work. It's a gross interference."

It is indeed.

"How can we be hunted for loving each other? We're not criminals."

Seems terribly unfair.

"I can live without friends ... but not without you."

She falls into my arms and weeps a little. I wrap myself gently around her.

"This has to end. We must push back somehow."

I stare helplessly at the wet sand. *It will require some thought.*

A big sigh. "Where are we?"

On the biggest island, unsurprisingly called Langkawi Island, a place said to inspire love and miracles.

"Perfect timing. And those buildings?"

That is the Berjaya Resort. We'll stay in a water chalet overlooking Burau Bay.

We jump for an aerial view. A stunning white sandy beach replete with numerous wooden umbrellas and deck chairs ... chalets hugging the coast and flowing into the trees … all cocooned in a vast rainforest with a mountain backdrop.

"Awesome, as usual." Her smile lights up my world.

The excess pearls mean zero financial worries. After perusing our new home we walk to the shops and find Lailah some clothes and swimwear. Soon we are gazing at the cobalt-blue sea from our private balcony.

Let's take it easy for the rest of the day.

"Says you. See you in the water!"

Soon we are splashing and cavorting … tumbling and kissing … lying on the beach under a warm sun, a gentle breeze flapping the corners of our towels.

After a couple of blissful hours I venture a niggling question. *Doesn't it bother you that I cannot physically experience you?*

"You're sharing my energies, right?"

Yes … I just sometimes wish there was more of a bridge between our worlds.

"Where did that come from?"

You think it too.

She hesitates, slowly tracing a circle in the soft sand.

"I don't believe in perfect lives or perfect relationships. That's unrealistic and naive. My dreams came true when you revealed yourself. I celebrate the good stuff and accept the challenges."

What good stuff?

"Really? Where shall I start? You are an angel. You radiate divine energy because you live close to the Source. Your own energy essence is particularly attractive to me – no one on earth makes me feel like you do. We travel anywhere instantly, live on paradisiacal beaches and dive in the deepest oceans. And you love me ... care for me ... protect me."

Is that enough?

"All I ever wanted was to be with you and to serve humanity. The rest is details."

Still ...

"Hey, you have given up a lot for me. All that knowledge, connection and belonging. It must be like losing your family."

I see what you see and hear what you hear ... and far more ... but I don't feel you when we touch, when we make love ...

"And I wonder what it feels like to surf energies."

Touché.

She is quiet for a while, then "You said you can be in many earthly places at once. Does that include other realms?"

Of course.

"Can you take me there one day?"

As a point of consciousness, yes, but not physically.

"Hmm ... What happens to my body if I go?"

It stays behind. Your physical body is merely an earth vehicle belonging to this dimension.

"That doesn't seem right."

I smile. *It is true for your current state of evolution.*

She rubs her chin. "So … from your position … you are a highly evolved being … pure consciousness … able to manifest in many realms, including the physical."

Yes, it's just a matter of perspective. Angels can shift their vibrational state and manifest downward into multitudinous realms.

"Why downward?"

It's a term of reference. You can manifest at any level you have transcended.

"Ah, it's a journey. Where are you going?"

The same place we are all going.

"To the Source?"

Indeed.

"Is that why there is a policy of non-interference? Each point of consciousness must evolve to the next level through its own experiences and choices?"

Yes. You cannot force an evolutionary jump. You can only hint, casually suggest and lead by example. All evolution is created by individual consciousness. It cannot come from outside.

"Rather like a plant that grows, irrespective of the sun and rain."

Exactly. Although the sun and rain help too.

"Wait a minute. Aren't Guardians bound to the earth plane?"

Laughter ripples through me. *It's just a title … and I no longer adhere to the rules of the job.*

"Oh." A glance at the horizon. "It's going to be dark soon. Will you take me to dinner?"

Sure.

We walk back to the chalet and she changes into a lovely mauve dress. Then we amble to the Pahn-Thai Restaurant which boasts innovative Thai cuisine. I offer the usual excuses to the waiter then watch her enjoying the meal. I guess there are some experiences we will never share.

* * *

Langkawi is an amazing place. In June 2007 the 99 islands of the archipelago were given World Geopark status by the United Nations Educational, Scientific and Cultural Organization. UNESCO defines a Geopark as 'a territory encompassing one or more sites of scientific importance, not only for geological reasons but also by virtue of its archaeological, ecological or cultural value'.

The reason? At 550 million years old, the Machinchang mountain range is one of the oldest rock formations in South East Asia. The ancient rainforests, teeming with exotic flora and fauna, are over 100 million years old.

Berjaya Resort is conveniently located a short drive from a cable-car system that travels all the way up Mount Machinchang. Lailah and I head out in the morning to the base station located at the Oriental Village shopping mall. We catch the Sky Cab and alight at the intermediate station, allowing us to enjoy a nature trek called Sky Trail that winds through the lush forests. It is utterly beautiful.

In the late afternoon the Sky Cab takes us to the top station. A short walk up the stairs and we are greeted by an astounding 125-metre curved suspension bridge known as the Sky Bridge. It hangs securely about 100 metres above the tree tops with a viewing platform at each end, offering spectacular panoramic views across the mountain. A truly captivating experience.

Back on the ground we grab a light meal at the Dayang Cafe then spend the evening relaxing in our chalet. With the busyness of the day easing, and refreshing sea air drifting across the room, Lailah curls up on the sofa and is quickly asleep.

She awakens to a splendid sunrise, the dawn rays streaming cheerfully onto the blanket. A yawn and stretch announce her presence.

Sleep well?

A slow nod. "I don't even remember dreaming."

Coffee?

"Please."

We stare out over the azure waters of Burau Bay.

Do you feel like visiting the south of the island today?

"What's there?"

Dataran Lang, or Eagle Square, which is located at Kuah Town beside the Kuah Jetty. There is a huge statue of 12-metre sea eagle with outstretched wings. We can also view the fountains, ponds and bridges, and walk around the town.

"Sounds fun. What's the significance of the eagle?"

Langkawi means 'reddish brown eagle' in colloquial Malay and there is an abundance of them on the islands.

"Interesting."

After breakfast we jump instantly and land unnoticed near one of the retail outlets. We spend some time shopping for more clothes then amble through the city, enjoying the wonderful sights.

In the afternoon we tour the white sandy beaches that fringe the coast and beckon the tourists. It's a strange contrast to the rest of the island which is mostly rural landscape with villages and paddy fields.

Eventually we bounce back to the deck chairs near our chalet. A waiter takes a drink and snack order from Lailah. We settle down to watch the receding sun softly soothing the horizon.

Don't you get lonely sometimes, sweetheart? I mean, it's just me all day and passers-by.

"Not really." She shrugs. "I guess everyone is different. Some people are social creatures, desiring a wide range of relationships and activities. For me, the romantic relationship is most important."

I nod.

"Besides, my life is a little unusual. No memories before the age of ten. A few years with foster parents. Then striding into the world on my own, working and studying."

I remember.

She bites her lip thoughtfully. "I studied psychology and have considered the rational explanations for my personality. The truth is I am different to most people. I have never felt like I belong in this world. Always felt like I came from somewhere else. So it's hard to make connections with ordinary human beings."

I understand.

"A stranger in a strange land." She shrugs again. "Hard to explain really."

Uh huh.

"Yours is the only energy that has drawn me. I always knew you were there."

The conversation drifts into a restaurant and disappears under a cosy blanket. As the night gently caresses her eyes I wonder to myself: How is it that two socially isolated beings, who don't seem to belong anywhere, get on so well? Why are we so happy together?

I notice the breeze wafting through the coconut palms and tenderly teasing the sea. My consciousness begins to meander among the bright stars.

Perhaps it will all make sense one day.

* * *

Over the next two months we explore Langkawi and the surrounding islands.

It turns out that Berjaya Resort is well positioned for the majority of our excursions. We head out to Sungai Kilim Nature Park, a protected mangrove swamp area, and discover uninhabited beaches and serene lagoons. Our ambling along the quiet river banks is accompanied by brown-winged kingfishers, monitor lizards and swimming macaque monkeys.

We visit Langkawi Bird Paradise and become immersed in the twitters and caws of more than 2,500 birds. A trip to Underwater World reveals over 5,000 varieties of fish, including sharks, stingray and huge turtles, all cruising idly behind clear glass walls.

Telaga Tujuh, which is part of the Mount Machinchang Forest Reserve, offers a lovely walk in verdant surroundings. It is not long before we stumble upon the seven wells – vertical tiers along which the mountain stream flows before cascading into a delightful waterfall.

We jump to the Lake of the Pregnant Maiden on one of the southern islands and gaze in awe at the undulating green hills that encircle the placid emerald waters.

Life settles into a comfortable coalescence of wild splashing, sunset walks, ocean dives, treatments at the local spa, candlelit dinners and downtime at the chalet.

One afternoon we are walking through the mangrove to reach a lovely secluded beach. It's the rustle that first disturbs me. Then the feeling that we are being watched. We quicken our pace. A red-eyed monkey swings from a tree, screeching loudly. Chasers! We run toward a shaded alcove, positioning the rock wall behind us. Within seconds we are surrounded by the entire troop. No way out.

Silent stand-off.

The Icelandic church flashes in my mind. That sudden shift in consciousness. I know what to do but it must be on my terms.

I whisper tenderly. *Lay down and relax in my energy field.*

Leaving just enough energy to protect Lailah's body, I grab her essence and make the jump. We are going to my world.

* * *

It's good to be home.

All around us the familiar green shimmer and the toing and froing of white-yellow energy sparks. I keep Lailah close and help her adjust to the foreign environment. My destination is the Sacred Temple where the Keepers of the Light reside. I aim to float on the steps until someone important listens to our case.

"I've been here before."

Hmm?

"This is not strange at all. I know this place."

Perhaps the shock of transition is confusing her.

She looks down at her body. "My true nature! At last."

Her energy field is showing bliss and peace. I am surprised.

We reach the temple and hover by the huge pillars. I can see the sparkling white-mauve essences of a couple of Overseers in the distance. I wonder what happened to the Chasers.

"There is no sound here. It's amazing. Are we communicating without words? Yes, we are."

Everything is a thought-force. An instant transmission of energy and intent.

"No sound … no touch … I can see your essence … naked and transparent … such sadness and defiant anger."

I see you too.

"You are not really a follower of conventions."

We are way past any rules.

"Oh … to know you like this … it's beautiful."

I have always known you like this.

I flow my essence to hug her.

Flickers of white-red energy. Chasers finally catching up. Overseers approaching.

Wow. That luminous energy field! So bright ... green, silver and gold ... everything is slowing down ... what's happening?

Come with me.

The hummingbird I saw fly out the temple window! After all this time! I have often wondered if it was just my imagination.

I have cloaked your energy fields, rendering you invisible on the energy grid.

Lailah's essence is enraptured. Joy flows through her.

"Invisible to whom?"

Every being in this world.

"Even the Keepers of the Light?"

They do not interfere in such matters.

"Oh ..."

Hmm, it's not clear to me either.

We drift to one of the extensive recreational areas. These differ from the sanctuaries and healing gardens which are often graced by newly ascended souls.

What is known and what is not known.

Being out of my depth, I decide that silence is the best option.

"Who are you?" asks Lailah, somewhat impertinently.

An Avatar. To answer your next question: An appearance or manifestation of the Source.

I can't resist. *Isn't everything a manifestation of the Source?*

Indeed.

Ok, this is going to be challenging.

I live beyond the systems.

"You don't belong here."

I don't belong anywhere.

"Sounds lonely."

My essence inclines me to certain choices. Every choice comes with a price.

"I understand."

Avatars are the catalysts of the universe. We like to flap our wings into established systems, especially ones that are working well.

"Aha."

As you can imagine, we are only mildly tolerated by most entities. Fortunately we are exceptionally powerful.

The hint of a smile permeates my energy field.

Here's the thing: You two have broken a lot of rules. Lailah shouldn't even be here.

I look away, slightly embarrassed.

My protection will not last long. This space is just a moratorium, a chance for you to gather your thoughts and make some decisions.

"What decisions?"

Your options are limited. Either I surrender Michael to the Overseers or he can choose to fall. Rules are there for a reason.

"Will the Overseers send me back to earth and prevent me from seeing Michael?"

Of course. It is in the best interests of everyone. Whatever happens, you, Lailah, will be returning shortly.

"Please. I don't want to lose him."

What do you mean by 'fall'?

You choose to become human. Your intention directs your energy. Once your hold your intention strongly, you will fall onto the earth plane and become a Walker.

I've never heard of such beings.

"Will he forfeit his powers?"

He will be completely human, just like you. With all the limitations. And no memory of his previous existence. A blank slate. A fresh start.

"No memories?"

Oh yes ... before you fall, remember to choose an age and gender.

"A gender?"

Angels have no gender or physical characteristics. That's a human projection. They are pure energy and pure consciousness.

"But he appears male to me."

You are comfortable with that facade. He can manifest in a myriad ways.

"Oh."

I suggest you take a walk to that big rock. You can see the earth from there. My protection will wear off soon.

"Where are you going? I have so many questions."

What is known and what is not known.

The hummingbird disappears.

"Michael, I'm scared."

I encircle her with my energy. We walk to the rock. Below us is a sheer drop into a dark abyss. The earth glimmers in the far distance.

It seems I either lose you or my life.

The quietness steadily envelops us.

"You can't give up your life for me."

The agony of the decision.

"I won't allow it."

Her essence reaches close and swirls into me. "Stay here, Michael. Live your life. Know that I will always love you."

She leaps into the chasm.

Lailah! No! No! What are you doing?

In that moment she looks back at me. I see the love in her eyes. I feel my essence rip apart. My mind begins screaming. A greater agony wrestles me to the ground.

What is my life worth? I can't live without her love. I can't live without her!

The protective energy field begins to shear. My exposure is imminent.

This decision has been edging toward me ever since I first met Lailah.

Those words sparkle in my mind ... 'It really is worth fighting for, being brave for, risking everything for. And the trouble is, if you don't risk anything, you risk even more.'

The protective field dissipates. Male, 28.

I fall into the abyss.

* * *

Blackness.

Sliver of light.

Disorientation. Fear.

Blackness. Light. Rock wall. Greenery.

I scream. So loud. Cover my ears. I have ears.

Touch my body. I am solid. Feels ... peculiar ...

"Michael."

Familiar blonde curls cascading upon me.

"Michael."

That voice. I know it. I know that voice!

"Michael, talk to me."

I slur … grunt … gravelly sound. Is that coming from me?

Soft hands caressing me … such pleasant sensations …

Laaailaahh.

"You remember me?"

I blink a few times.

"Michael?"

My name is Michael. And this is Lailah. I sit up and touch her cheek.

Moving my tongue, wiggling my jaw. *Lailah.*

"That's better."

She clambers onto me and holds me in a deep embrace.

"I love you, you crazy stupid man."

Something fires inside me.

I love you too, Lailah.

"You do? You remember us?"

I nod. Then shake my head.

I know you. I feel you. You are part of me.

"You forgot the details?"

I look at her blankly.

"Come on. Let's go home."

Standing ... slowly ... heavy body ... unstable ... shaking legs ... walking ...

How much further?

"It's only been ten minutes."

This body is so uncoordinated.

"We'll get a taxi once we exit the mangrove."

Why do I know some things but cannot recall others?

"You know the names of things?"

Uh huh.

"You know you love me?"

Yes.

"Well, that's a good start."

My nose tickles.

"Your sense of smell."

Mmm ... your scent is sweet and lovely.

"Thank you."

She kisses me on the cheek.

Wow.

We stumble past the trees and hail a taxi. The driver looks at me strangely. Soon we arrive at a gorgeous chalet overlooking shimmering blue water.

We live here?

"We do. Now go have a shower."

I sniff. *Is that smell coming from me?*

"Oh yeah."

I find the bathroom and look in the mirror. Unkempt long dark hair, green eyes, unshaven. My body is lithe and slightly muscular with an olive skin. Who is this person looking back at me?

Do you have a razor I can use?

"In the cabinet."

What a glorious feeling. All steam and warm rivulets. Great aromas. Fresh and invigorating. *Hey, I love this. Gonna do it every day!*

"I hope so."

Dry off and walk to the sofa.

Lailah is staring at me. "Wow, good choice."

Huh?

She starts kissing me all over. Touching ... stroking ... creating ripples of pleasure ... warm mouth and sensual lips ... her soft body wrapping around me. I stare into her sky-blue eyes. We fit perfectly together ... spectacular sensations ... gradual rising of energy ... flowing ... merging ... overwhelming ...

I shout her name. Her sweet voice blends with mine. Waves of blissful nothingness.

My heart swirls with tenderness ... drawing her close ... cuddling and gazing at each other.

I love you, Lailah.

"I love you too."

* * *

"Hey, sleepyhead ..."

What happened? Where am I?

"You've been asleep for twelve hours."

Is that a lot?

"It is for most people."

My stomach feels uncomfortable.

"You need to eat. I made a fruit salad. Take it slow ... it's your first meal."

It is?

"There is so much to tell you."

A deluge of flavours and scents. My mouth is drowning in a delicious world.

We take a walk on the beach. The soft sand runs between my toes and tickles my feet. A sea breeze teases my long hair. Warm sunlight caresses my skin. I take a few deep invigorating breaths.

Lailah, this is fabulous! Is this heaven?

She gives me a strange look. "Sit here with me."

For the next hour I get a fantastic update. Hard to believe. I stand up and stretch then run into the expansive ocean. The long swim allows me to consider the story.

Apparently I am an angel in a human body. All memories of my previous existence were wiped clean so I could start again. So that we could enjoy love and freedom.

She also explained that my home is a blissful place located near to the Source. Run by a hierarchy of powerful spiritual entities. At the top, concealed in a sacred temple, are beings that burn so bright that it is impossible to look upon them. These Keepers of the Light are closely connected to the Source. The administrators and rule enforcers are called Overseers. Messengers and Guardians are the teachers and guides who work in many worlds. Chasers are Messengers who have been granted special powers to rein in errant behaviour.

And on the lowest rung are the Walkers. Incarnated angels. Beings who once had supreme knowledge and power but now are as limited as the humans they walk among.

I am a 28-year-old man named Michael. No history, no birth certificate, no identity.

Stumbling out the water, I find Lailah and join her on the deck chairs.

I know it's the truth. It resonates deep inside me.

She nods thoughtfully.

My only question is: What now?

"The same question that faces every human on this earth."

Touché.

"We are free to create any life we choose. To explore, discover, evolve."

When did you become so wise?

She winks at me. "I had a great mentor."

We pack up with laughter. What an absurd situation. A beautiful woman and a fallen angel. And an entire life laying open before us.

"Would you like to try ice cream?"

Yeah. Bring it on.

We interlace our fingers and amble across the warm sand. It seems there is an adventure of the senses waiting for me. I glance at the loving companion by my side. We will share this journey through life together. That's the most important thing of all.

* * *

"I want to move to Hawaii."

You don't like it here anymore?

"I do. But we need to build a new life. I am a US citizen. You love the oceans and warm climate. It seems like a good fit."

Tell me more about the weather.

"Hawaii has a warm tropical climate with summer highs of 32 degrees Celsius, dropping to about 26 degrees during the winter. And the near-constant trade winds from the east tend to offset the temperature and humidity."

I nod. *Suits me perfectly.*

"We can charter a boat from Malaysia. The route navigates along the South China Sea and then east across the Pacific."

Sounds like you have a plan.

Lailah sketches a map in the sand.

"Hawaii is the 50th US state and the only one comprised entirely of islands. Hundreds of islands in fact, spread out over 2,400 kilometres. At the south-eastern end of the archipelago are eight main islands: Niihau, Kauai, Oahu, Molokai, Lanai, Kahoolawe, Maui and the island of Hawaii. The latter is also known as the Big Island to avoid confusion with the state name. We can explore these eight and decide where we want to settle."

Do you have any preferences?

"The Big Island contains active volcanoes. Oahu is the most populous and the location of the capital Honolulu. It is probably too busy for quiet people like us but I would like to be near it."

Where are the best beaches?

"Running north to south: Kauai, Oahu and Maui."

How do you know all this?

She sighs, a hint of sadness in her voice. "I lived on Oahu from the age of ten until twenty-two. It's when I first became aware of you."

I cannot remember.

"It will be like coming home for us."

That stings slightly but I say nothing. Her drawing shows Kauai situated just north of Oahu.

Kauai looks good.

"It does. Are you alright with me organising everything?"

Sure.

Two weeks later we are passengers on a huge yacht. It turns out that we are seriously wealthy because of Lailah's unusual pearls. The captain and crew are most attentive.

We disembark at Puako Bay on the north side of the Big Island, which is the southernmost of the eight main islands, transferring to a small boat then to a waiting car. The Mauna Kea Beach Hotel welcomes us in traditional Hawaiian style. A glossy pamphlet at the reception informs us about the gorgeous ocean views, great restaurants, spa, swimming pool, 18-hole championship golf course and 11 tennis courts.

Perhaps it is time I learned a sport, I whisper as we are checking in.

"Wow, you are turning into a real man."

Am I different to how I used to be?

"Same essence inside. That's what I love."

As we walk to our room I wonder if this is hard for Lailah. Perhaps I am different. It is uncomfortable having no personal memories but I also have no memories of the time we shared. It's like a chunk of our lives is missing. On top of this, I have no idea who I am or what I am doing with my life.

The room is spacious with a lovely king-size bed. I leap onto it and bounce softly. On the wall is a large portrait of Leo Tolstoy with a quote from his book War and Peace: 'The strongest of all warriors are these two – Time and Patience'.

I have to smile. Everything is going to be alright.

* * *

Our new life begins with an exploration of the eight main islands. The Big Island is a phenomenon of varying climate zones and great biodiversity, where lush rainforests flow into volcanic deserts and snow-capped mountains form a backdrop to beautiful black and green sand beaches.

We start our journey at Hawaii Volcanoes National Park, the largest park in the state. The Big Island is entirely formed by volcanic activity and comprises: five coalesced volcanoes (Kilauea – the most active volcano on earth; Mauna Loa – active – the largest volcano on earth; Hualalai – active; Mauna Kea – dormant; Kohala – extinct); one submarine volcano that has already subsided below sea level (Mahukona); and one submarine volcano that has yet to grow to sea level (Loihi).

The park offers 240 kilometres of hiking trails so Lailah and I decide to spend the week meandering along the wondrous walks. It gives us the chance to experience the ever-changing natural environment. On the fourth day we stumble across an enormous petroglyph field. The guide book indicates that we are standing at the sacred Puuloa Petroglyphs, a display of over 23,000 ancient images carved into the surrounding lava rock.

"Michael, have a look at this."

What is it?

She points at the ground. "Look ..."

I stare at the rock. *An etching of two winged beings.*

"Isn't that crazy?"

A reflection of truth. That's how these myths get started.

"And over here."

A hummingbird.

"Hawaii does not have hummingbirds."

That is definitely a hummingbird.

"And a large flaming circle. The sun?"

Probably the Light ... the Source ...

"Aha."

I wonder what secrets are hidden in these carvings.

She scampers across the grass.

"These shimmering pillars ... must be the Sacred Temple."

Sacred temple?

"Remember, the one I told you about?"

I sigh. *Oh yeah.*

"And these small footprints surely represent the Walkers."

How is it that you remember my world and I don't?

"You fell and amnesia is part of the deal. I was only visiting."

My fingers trace the line of a footprint. *Hmm ...*

She puts her arm around me. "You ok?"

Do you think there is an overarching plan? Or are we creating reality?

"I don't know. What about the policy of non-interference?"

What policy?

We burst into laughter.

She grabs my hand. "Come on. Let's get back to walking. There's so much to explore."

* * *

This morning we are up before dawn. We are joining a boat trip that departs from Isaac Hale Beach Park near Pahoa and cruises down the Kalapana coast.

Every day for more than 25 years Kilauea Volcano has pumped masses of red hot lava into the ocean, creating blistering fountains of steam and volcanic debris. The best time to view this magnificent spectacle is at sunrise or sunset and our experienced captain has promised us front row seats.

With the boat anchored at a safe distance we watch the flowing molten magma and explosive interactions. It's a fiery reminder of nature's power.

Afterward we sail slowly back as scintillating rays sweep over the horizon. I cuddle close to Lailah and gaze upon the illuminated ocean. It's wonderful sharing this adventure with the woman I love.

Over the next few days we visit the Akaka Falls and Wailuku River State Parks and enjoy the gorgeous waterfalls and bubbling pools; amble along the manicured pathways and lagoons of the Liliuokalani Japanese Gardens; and tour a couple of coffee farms in Kona, taking care to sample their delicious products.

And finally my beloved beaches. The popular white sand beaches with their calm waters are found along the west coast; the black and green ones are located on the southern shores. We are laying here watching the rippling surf and basking under the soothing sun. The Big Island has been done; great for tourism but not where we want to settle.

Nonetheless, Lailah has made a great choice. Hawaii is going to be a fabulous place to live.

* * *

Next stop, Maui. The guide book calls it the Magic Isle and for good reason.

We commence with a road journey along the rugged eastern coastline which presents incredible views of the lush rainforests and rolling ocean. The following day we hire horses and explore Haleakala National Park and the tranquil tiered Pools of Oheo. Haleakala means 'house of the sun' and is the highest peak in Maui, offering spectacular views across the island. The rich volcanic soil of Kula on the slopes of Haleakala provides ideal conditions for farming; soon we are immersed in the rich fragrances and colours of Alii Kula Lavender Farm, Shim Protea Farm and Kula Botanical Gardens.

In central Maui we survey the emerald peaks of Iao Valley State Park and hike the trail until we find the 365-metre-high Iao Needle, an iconic green-mantled rock outcropping. We travel to west Maui and discover dozens of art galleries and 5 kilometres of white sand called Kaanapali Beach. In the evening we watch the enthralling sunset cliff-diving ceremony that takes place daily at the beach's northernmost cliffs. Then we traipse to Merriman's restaurant, home of Hawaii Regional Cuisine and the 'farm to table' concept, and relish a delectable dinner.

Lailah wants to introduce me to the island's famous surf spots so the next few days are spent relaxing on the gentle beaches of Kaanapali, Lahaina, Kihei, Hookipa and Honolua Bay, and gaping in awe at the big wave surfing in Peahi. The surfers seem to move with such grace and ease, carving serenely through formidable rollers.

So peaceful ... soulful ... a direct connection to nature ...

She smiles knowingly. "It is much harder than it looks."

I think it's an activity that will suit my temperament.

"Sign up for lessons. We're here for a while."

I saunter to the surf shop and organise my afternoon. My thoughts drift to Lailah. Things are feeling a bit different. Something is shifting. There is a distance growing between us. I must ask her about this.

A long yellow finless board lies underneath me on the sand. The group is practising the jump position ... over and over ... paddle, push up, jump ... paddle, push up, jump ... Finally we attach our foot-leashes and try our luck in the small waves. What follows is a series of hilarious and fun tumbles. It seems impossible to stay on the board for more than a few seconds.

At the end of the day I drag my exhausted body into an invigorating shower. Then we grab a takeaway dinner, repose on the beach and watch the sunset.

Is everything alright with us, sweetheart?

"Why do you ask?"

You seem quieter.

"I'm just getting used to you."

Have I changed that much?

"Thing is … before, you were pure energy unadulterated by earthly influences. Now you are in a male body subject to the effects of testosterone and a masculine brain."

I look at her quizzically.

"I am starting to understand that a person is made up of their spiritual essence plus the effects of inherited human genetics, temperament and hormones."

Please explain.

"You chose a male body. And it is filtering your essence. I guess this happens to all beings who incarnate on the earth plane."

How am I different from when we first met?

"You still have the same beautiful essence. I am still in love with you."

Good to hear. Answer the question.

"We are both quiet people but you seem to be in your own world a lot more. You don't share your thoughts as much. And you are more task-focused, less able to sit still …"

I frown and brush the sand off my feet. *I have noticed that. This body-mind seeks activity, doing, achieving.*

"You used to lay and stare at the night sky for hours while I slept."

Can't imagine …

"Exactly."

I need to learn about this body-mind so we can evolve our relationship together.

"You seem to wake late in the mornings. How about surfing in the afternoons and making time for us in the evenings?"

It's a deal.

"I love you very much, my strange fallen angel."

I love you too, my darling.

The new day brings a sunrise full of promise. We share an enormous bowl of fruit salad consisting of diced bananas, java plums, mangos, guavas, passion fruit, mountain apples, pineapples, papaya and lychees. It's a delicious and healthy breakfast that leaves me brimming with energy.

I switch to private lessons to speed up my learning. The instructor has a video camera to record the session. Afterward we have a good laugh watching me being mangled by the waves. He encourages me: "The only way you achieve anything is with knowledge, tutorship and practice, practice, practice."

As I stroll away, the conversation lingers in my mind. Wise words indeed.

Lailah and I are relaxing in the twilight with cocktails. The ocean is gently swooshing and a delightful warmth is breezing across our clothes.

Tell me more about the influence of these human bodies.

She shrugs. "Everything comes from the field of relationship psychology. I studied it at university and stayed up to date with developments."

Ok, I'm interested.

"Hmm ... Where shall we start? Sociological differences between men and women are lessening. We see this in equal suffrage, equal opportunities, equal pay for similar work, and so forth. And this is as it should be."

Agreed.

"However, there are tremendous biological and neurological differences between men and women, largely due to hormones and brain wiring. These differences are amplified by the divergent ways boys and girls are socialised by parents, school, society, culture and the media."

How does that affect relationships?

"Men and women have dissimilar ways of processing information and communicating, disparate sensory prominence, and distinct orientations toward tasks and relationships."

Is that true for all humans?

"Not exactly. That's a general classification for most humans. Hormone levels and brain wiring vary per individual, resulting in a range of possibilities: feminine men, masculine women, gay persons, and so forth."

Ah, richness in diversity.

She smiles. "I like that." Fingers stroke her arm thoughtfully. "Understanding the general differences between the genders will help our romantic and social relationships immensely."

Why don't they teach this in schools?

She rolls her eyes. "Now that is a dream." A brief pause. "The secret is to move beyond the mere accepting of differences. We need to understand the opposite gender's ingrained perspective and learn to speak their language."

You seem to have given this some thought.

"Indeed. I call it Love Whispering."

I gaze into her eyes and smile.

That's beautiful, Lailah.

* * *

The bright sun is streaming through the bedroom window. I blink my eyes lazily. Lailah ambles in with two breakfast trays and seats herself next to me.

"Sleep well?"

As always. I arrange the pillows. *I love sleeping. Dreams are great adventures.*

"Where shall we go next? Lanai is just a hop from Maui."

What's there?

"Nothing much. It is known as the Most Secluded Island. It's a place to get away from city living and stress. You can 4x4 along the rustic 21-kilometre Munro Trail, view acrobatic spinner dolphins at Hulopoe Bay and visit Sweetheart Rock near Manele Bay."

Can we save that for our honeymoon?

"Are you serious?"

Hmm?

"Our honeymoon!" She smacks me on the shoulder.

I laugh. *You haven't thought about it?*

"Don't mess with me. I'm a traditional girl when it comes to marriage."

You want me to propose?

"When the time is right – absolutely!"

And a ring?

"White gold with a mounted pearl – from my necklace."

Sounds perfect.

"I take it we are skipping Lanai?"

Yes please.

"How about Molokai, the island north of Maui?"

I smile. *What's on offer?*

"The tallest sea cliffs in the world; Papohaku, Hawaii's longest white sand beach; and the trails of Kalaupapa National Park and Halawa Valley."

I think we've kinda been there, done that.

"Well, that leaves my home island as our next destination."

Oahu?

"Yep."

You going to charter a private boat?

"Uh huh."

Cool.

We finish breakfast and Lailah makes some calls. She comes bounding in. "Few people are willing to make the journey as the channel is quite rough. But I found someone with a large sturdy boat who is leaving in two hours."

I run my fingers through my hair. *It's a good thing we travel light. I'll have a quick shower.*

"Whoo hoo! Time to move."

Her excitement is contagious. I notice little butterflies flitting in my stomach. Soon we are out the door and waiting at the dock. The voyage is relatively easy. As we approach Waikiki Yacht Club on the southern shore of Oahu, she announces "We're home!"

We arrive at the sumptuous Kahala Hotel and stow our gear. The phone rings in our room. *It's the concierge. Apparently our taxi is waiting.*

Lailah smiles. "Hope you like surprises."

The taxi delivers us to Blue Hawaiian Helicopters near Honolulu International Airport. During the briefing we are introduced to the state-of-the-art quiet-technology Eco-Star helicopter, featuring spacious individual seats, noise-cancelling headsets, and expansive glass for exceptional visibility.

It's an awesome way to show off the island. The tour takes us over the turquoise waters of Waikiki; the extinct volcano of Diamond Head; crescent-shaped Hanauma Bay; the white sands of Waimanalo beach; Chinaman's Hat; and the beautiful coral formations of Kaneohe Bay. We fly over the cliffs of Nuuanu Valley rainforest; along the breathtaking coastline to Sacred Falls and Dole Pineapple Plantation; finishing with sweeping views of Pearl Harbour, Arizona Memorial and Battleship Missouri.

I grab Lailah's hand. *That was marvellous! Thank you.*

Over the next few days we take a walking tour which includes Iolani Palace, the official residence of the Hawaiian Kingdom's last two monarchs from 1882 to 1893; Aliiolani Hale, a building housing the Hawaii State Supreme Court, in front of which is a statue of King Kamehameha I, the great warrior, diplomat and leader who united the Hawaiian Islands into one royal kingdom in 1810; the State Capitol building and Washington Place; the historic Kawaiahao Church; and the Mission Houses Museum and State Art Museum. We also visit the tranquil Honolulu Botanical Gardens.

"How are you liking it so far?" she asks one morning.

It's a fabulous place. Living here would be wonderful.

"But wait ... there's more."

I burst into laughter. *You're a walking advertisement for Oahu.*

She pouts. "This might be our new home. I want you to see everything."

No worries. What's next?

"Snorkelling at the stunning Hanauma Bay, just up the road."

Oh yeah. I'm in.

We rent masks, snorkels and fins and head out for the day. A notice explains that this is a Marine Life Conservation District and emphasises that visitors must preserve the fragile marine ecosystem. Prohibitions include littering and touching the sea animals or coral. Hovering along the surface we carefully navigate the clear blue waters, occasionally diving deep to explore the lively reefs and colourful fish. It is a serene and delightful experience.

The following morning Lailah is rhythmically swaying to an evocative melody. She looks over at my curious face. "Hula is a form of Hawaiian dance. It dramatizes a song or chant."

Ah, thanks for explaining.

She ruffles my hair affectionately. "Can you handle another day in the water?"

Sure.

"You're gonna love this one."

Tell me.

"There is a private lagoon right next to the hotel where we can swim with dolphins."

Awesome!

"Another option is an excursion to Ko Olina on the southwest coast to snorkel with wild dolphins and sea turtles."

Let's stroll to the lagoon.

An hour later, compulsory life jackets donned, we are treading water under the watchful eye of the trainer. Time is spent getting to know the Atlantic Bottlenose dolphins in shallow water and Lailah is lucky enough to receive a kiss. Soon we are mingling underwater with these magnificent marine creatures. I am awed by their grace and intelligence and soulful smiles.

There is a sudden shearing of my consciousness. A cascade of memories. Deep ocean. Darkening blue. Dolphins. Pearls. Coral reefs. What's happening? I thrust my head out the water and take a few breaths.

"Are you ok, honey?"

I don't know. Just had a flashback. Done this before ... diving in the ocean ... many times ...

"Wow. You are starting to remember."

Is that possible?

"Maybe your angel consciousness is seeping into your human mind."

A whole other life is hidden from me ...

I watch Lailah playing for a while then move to the water's edge. Another half hour and our session is complete.

"Shall we go down to the beach?"

That sounds good.

We spend the rest of the day watching the rippling waves from the comfortable perch of our deck chairs, blissfully sipping ice-cold drinks and chatting about nothing in particular. It's a welcome distraction from cogitating on my missing memories.

* * *

My eyelids flutter in the morning light.

Had the most vivid surreal dream.

She cuddles in close. "Yeah?"

All turquoise and white. Floating ... drifting ... a hummingbird with green, silver and gold plumage ...

"Did you say 'hummingbird'?"

Uh huh.

"That's the hummingbird!"

The one in your story?

"It's not a story. It's the truth."

I know.

"Maybe it's a sign."

Of what?

She shrugs. "No idea. Something is happening."

I stare out the window and sigh.

Lailah places her hand on mine. "If it's any consolation, I get little snatches of my missing years too."

You do?

"Yep, but I never know what is real. Is it a dream? Is it my imagination?"

Why would it be your imagination?

"Because they are not earthly memories ... glimpses of travelling through space ... soaring among the stars ... visiting strange and wonderful planets ..."

Really?

"Yes."

That is weird.

"Hey, I don't criticise your memories."

No, I mean it is weird that you don't see your childhood.

"Oh ... that never happens."

It's all a mystery. I'm going to shower.

"May I join you?"

Absolutely. Wash my back?

"Wash mine?"

Deal.

Laughter, song and swirling steam fill the bathroom.

After breakfast I make a suggestion. *Let's go to the Wet 'n Wild water park in Kapolei.*

"Excellent idea. Did you see the pamphlet? So many fabulous rides."

Oh yeah. Swim shorts – check. Sunscreen – check. Fruit salad, cooler box – check. Ready to rock 'n roll?

A quick journey, through the entrance and the first leap into the water. "Whoo hoo!" All around us the echo of joyful splashing and cavorting. The sun is shining brightly. It's a perfect day.

I loooooove the water slides! Race you to the top!

We grab an inflatable tube and fly down the Big Kahuna. Such fun! Then we twist and turn down the individual slides of the Waianae Coasters and hurtle along the Island Racers. A long session of bodysurfing in the huge wave pool saps the last of our excited energy.

"Let's chillax and watch the surfers at Da Flowrider."

Chill-what?

A big smile. "The youngsters are saying that. Chill and relax."

Aha.

We stroll across and find a couple of chairs in the shade. I open the cooler box and stretch out my arms. Gorgeous sun … clear blue skies … refreshing breeze … chillaxing by the rolling waters … this is the good life.

You know what would be great? Tell me more about those gender differences.

"Are you sure?"

I cannot reclaim my previous life so I may as well invest in this one.

"Sensible strategy."

Off you go.

"Bear in mind these are general differences. There are many individual variations."

Disclaimer acknowledged. Proceed.

"Ignoring your spiritual essence for the moment, a large part of 'who you are' is made up of genetics, hormones and socialisation."

Yep, got that.

"Your brain wiring is the result of thousands of years of species-experience. The contribution of your parents' and families' genes only overlays that ancient code."

So ... the deepest layer is the accumulated species-experience ... then personal genetic inheritance and hormones.

"Exactly. On one level we have all the masculine and feminine possibilities. However, in the very early stages of physiological development genes and hormones will create a gender bias. After that, socialisation will simply crystallise or modify that bias."

Gender bias means male or female brain wiring?

"Yes. Here are the general differences:

"Men usually define and value themselves predominantly through work, career, achievements and accomplishments. They need challenges and competition. Romantic love is merely a *part* of their lives. Women tend to define and value themselves mostly through their relationships. They need connection and co-operation. Romantic love and social relating permeate their *entire* lives."

Hmm ... I can see where conflict arises.

"Love Whispering involves understanding your partner's dispositions and operating within their framework. By necessity, this requires empathy, wisdom and loving compromise."

So a woman needs to pay attention and take an interest in a man's career and achievements, offering support and admiration where appropriate. And a man needs to be careful of too much task-focus and ensure he carves out time for loving connection with his woman.

"Now you're getting it."

Are there more differences?

"Of course. As a rule, men are more autonomous and less connecting than women, meaning they have less friends. You can imagine a man walking steadfastly along an arrow-line in pursuit of a goal whereas a woman is standing in the centre of expanding and overlapping circles. To bond with a man you need to walk an arrow-line together, by sharing an *activity*; to bond with a woman you need to join in those circles, by *talking*."

That picture helps me a lot.

She nods sagely. "I know."

So men, who tend to be introspective and quieter, need to converse more with their women. And women may choose to connect with their men by finding activities they can do together.

"Keeping in mind the arrow-line and overlapping circles: Men tend to seek freedom and space on their unwavering journey; women desire closeness, connection and intimacy."

Ouch, another conflict.

"That mismatch becomes dynamically amplified when a woman becomes demanding or intrusive. If a man feels his freedom or space is being threatened, he will usually physically retreat or emotionally disappear – the very opposite of what a woman desires. A woman should never chase her man; instead she makes it clear that she is available and wanting to connect, and then she moves away. The man must chase the woman."

Sounds like a golden rule.

"Absolutely. That rule underlies the majority of successful male-female interactions."

I tap my right temple. *Ok, storing it now.*

"A man who understands the art of Love Whispering will capitalise on his freedom but remember his woman's need for intimacy and closeness. He knows when to walk away from his mission and make time for bonding and connecting."

That's the kind of man I want to be.

She gives me a huge smile and squeezes my hand.

"Irrespective of gender bias, there needs to be a balance of closeness and independence in a relationship. If one partner is unfulfilled in some aspect of their life they may demand too much from the other partner in an effort to compensate. A partner cannot fulfil all your needs. Outside interests are essential, for example: own friends, work, social and recreational activities.

"As Kahlil Gibran wrote in his inspiring book The Prophet: '… let there be spaces in your togetherness, and let the winds of the heavens dance between you … and stand together yet not too near together: For the pillars of the temple stand apart, and the oak tree and the cypress grow not in each other's shadow.'"

Right, I'm off. See you later.

"Where are you going?"

I burst into laughter. *Just kidding.*

"You silly man!" She slaps my arm.

Seriously though. Are you ready for more play?

She nods. "Enough talking. More action."

Hey, that's man-speak.

"Love Whispering, my darling. Last one to the Surfsliders is a squishy banana."

Between the mirth and her quick start, I don't stand a chance. Panting, we meet at the top and hurl ourselves into the swirling water. Shrieks of exhilaration accompany our speedy descent. As we emerge from the splash pool I glance thoughtfully at Lailah. She is a wise and wonderful companion and I am grateful to be sharing my life with her.

By the evening we are both very tired. We settle for a candlelit dinner at the hotel then collapse onto our soft bed. I am asleep before my head touches the pillow.

* * *

A huge yawn welcomes the new day.

Nice. I can see your tonsils.

"Love you too, my darling."

I am no expert in Love Whispering but I know enough to start every morning with a cuddle. Women have yummy sensors sprinkled over every square centimetre of their bodies. Cuddling is as important as talking.

I don't feel like going anywhere. Can we have a quiet time by the pool?

"Suits me. I'll catch up on my reading."

Later in the morning we wander down and find a couple of deck chairs. All I want is a refreshing swim and to repose in the warm sun. We opt for a lazy lunch of light beer and speciality salads: spicy potato for me and Greek-avocado-quinoa for her. The afternoon is serene and restful.

Around 4pm I excuse myself and stroll over to the concierge. I am only gone for a few minutes. Lailah doesn't seem to notice.

Sweetheart?

"Hmm?"

I thought we could have dinner in our room tonight.

"Yes please."

The waiter will deliver everything at seven.

"Ok."

After an hour we leave the pool. Lailah enters the hotel room first and is quickly awed then delighted. "Michael! It's so romantic."

Rose petals are strewn across the floor, forming a trail from the lounge through to the bedroom. A bottle of champagne rests in an ice bucket. Chocolates and strawberries are nestled on the small table.

The cork pops and bubbly flows into the crystal flutes. I raise my glass. *To a lifetime of Love Whispering.*

"A lifetime of Love Whispering."

I draw her close and kiss her softly. My lips dance a slow samba across her delicate skin. I massage her back for a while then open the basket of delicacies. We drift into a dizzying melange of delectable scents and delicious flavours and luscious caresses ... gradually melting into each other ... surrendering into a sensual rhythm and love's sweet gaze ...

We laying cuddling for a long time ... then it's a quick shower.

Dinner arrives on schedule. Perfect. I'm starving.

* * *

Lailah wakens in a bright and breezy mood.

"Are you going to continue the surf lessons?"

Uh huh. Just been acclimatising to the new island.

"The best teachers here are the firefighters."

Are you serious?

"Yep. The Hawaiian Fire Surf School is owned and operated by Honolulu firefighters. They have great credentials and are naturally very fit and safety conscious."

Unusual combination.

She smiles. "The lessons are given at a secluded beach near Ko Olina. A barrier reef breaks down any large swells, creating optimal waves for surfing instruction."

Sounds good. What do I bring?

"They supply everything: surf board, leash, reef shoes, rash guard, shade tent and chairs. Pack your own lunch and water. Shall I phone and make a booking?"

Please. Will you be joining me?

She shakes her head. "There's a couple of old friends I'd like to meet. If there is a lesson available today, do you want to go?"

I nod. The words 'let there be spaces in your togetherness' flit into my consciousness. It's strange thinking of being apart from Lailah. We have spent every waking moment together for so long.

The Hawaiian Fire van collects me from the hotel and I join a small group of first-timers on the beach. It's a late morning lesson and soon everyone is toppling from their boards into the water. The experience lies somewhere between frustrating and hilarious.

I chat to the instructor and organise a week of private lessons. The only way to improve is through one-to-one coaching and lots of practice. I have the time and Lailah won't mind.

Over the next few days I learn about surfboards and surfing. A big wave gun board has long sweeping curved sides which enable long gentle turns. Shorter boards with more rounded curves turn tighter. A wide square tail allows more aggressive turns than a narrow pin tail or swallow tail. Fins have a huge impact on feel, stability, drive and manoeuvrability. A board can have from one to four fins. More fins make a board more stable; fewer fins make a board looser in the water and easier to turn. These days most fins are removable, making it easy to alter the type and/or number of fins on a board to suit varying surf conditions.

Surfing is such a peaceful sport. Quiet, flowing, and surrounded by sea, sun and fresh air. It's one part meditation and one part exhilaration. I adore it.

After a couple of weeks I notice a dramatic increase in my skill and confidence. Each small breakthrough leads to a greater feeling of mastery. I'm starting to get the hang of it. On the Friday afternoon Lailah shows up, kitted out and surfboard in hand. I bound over and give her a kiss.

Hey sweetheart, what you up to?

"Thought I'd join you today."

I smile. *You can surf? How come you never told me?*

She shrugs nonchalantly. "Didn't want you to feel pressure."

Hope I can keep up with you.

"That's exactly my point. Just be yourself."

Ok.

"I used to feel your presence alongside me when I was surfing. It was an amazing feeling."

Wish I could remember …

"It will probably come back to you."

Alright … let's carve some waves!

We dash into the sea and paddle out. I catch the first face and manage a good run. Standing in the shallow water I look for Lailah. After a few moments she's off. Wow, she's really good. I watch her fly into an aerial manoeuvre then snap the top of the wave. Impressive.

A couple of hours later we are back on the beach. There's still plenty of sun so we spread our towels on the warm sand and unzip the cooler box. Cold drinks and sandwiches – great sustenance for fatigued surfers.

"You feel like hearing more about the gender differences?"

I stretch out my body and relax. *Yeah. Go ahead.*

"Ok … The single greatest challenge facing most relationships is communication. Men and women have very different perception and communication styles. Cast your mind to our previous conversation."

Arrow-lines and overlapping circles?

She nods. "Women talk to connect and bond. Men talk in order to expedite goals. When men communicate, they are expressing and listening for succinct points to facilitate goal achievement."

So a man will listen to his woman's apparent rambling and wonder how it adds value to his mission. He thinks to himself 'What's the point of this conversation?' and he will become frustrated unless he remembers that conversations are also about companionship and sharing ideas.

"You're on fire. Have we discussed this before?"

I'm a man. I've had a few thoughts about the matter.

"A woman should also be sensitive to her man's achievement orientation. It can be helpful if she reminds him that he doesn't have to solve or accomplish anything during their conversation. Just being mentally present is enough."

That's a useful suggestion.

"Remember, our brains contain ancient operating codes that strongly influence the way we perceive and communicate. The masculine brain evolved to master the hunt: long-range strategic vision; mono-focus; solitary; internal thought-processing and problem-solving; direct and succinct communication aimed at attaining the goal."

Too much talking scares away the prey. Think it through, communicate briefly, then act. Arrow-line.

"The female brain evolved to master caring – especially toward children and other females while the men were away hunting: enhanced peripheral vision; multi-focus; community; conversation for thought-processing and problem-solving; indirect, unstructured and discursive communication aimed at bonding and connecting."

Houston, we have a problem.

"Yep. That's why we need empathy and wisdom when speaking to a romantic partner. We need to understand their brain profile and learn to speak their language."

Love Whispering. Now you're talking.

She smiles. "Great tag line."

Where to from here?

"Most communication issues stem from disparate brain profiles. For example, women use conversations to process thoughts, solve problems and de-stress. Consequently they talk a lot more than men. Men tend to internalise thinking and problem-solving, and they de-stress by reducing communication."

So after a hard day's work, the woman desperately needs to have a conversation while the man needs to sit quietly.

"Precisely. And in her world – community – lack of communication is unsettling and fosters insecurity and anxiety. In his world – hunting – too much communication, especially accompanied by strong emotion, equals danger. Those diverse negative emotions are enough to precipitate horrendous arguments."

Perhaps a man can be left alone for a while until he reaches equilibrium. Then he can put his full attention on his woman's conversational needs.

"What was that golden rule?"

Never chase a man. The woman makes it clear that she is available and wanting to connect. Then she moves away. He will search for her when he is ready.

"And then there's the contrasting focus issue. A woman's brain profile enables her to multi-task and multi-track. She can easily discuss several topics at the same time. A man has a limited and highly focused attention span. He tends to mono-task and mono-track, preferring to focus on one objective or one topic at a time. In addition, a woman seeks and expresses details in her conversations; a man seeks and expresses succinct facts."

So a woman should not throw too much information at a man. He will not remember it. If it's important, she can trim the message to a few simple points. Or draw him a picture. Equally, a man must remember that his woman enjoys hearing detailed information.

"The male brain is highly visual so that is actually a great idea."

No wonder men and women struggle to communicate.

"One last thing. The ancient hunting brain causes men to be more stoical and use less facial expressions when listening. This can confuse a woman as her female friends use a range of expressions and vocal tones."

I stare blankly at Lailah.

She slaps my arm and giggles. "Cute."

If a brain profile is a physiological disposition then it is very difficult to change.

"Love Whispering does not try to change the other person. It is about understanding their disposition and communicating in a profiled manner."

I really appreciate you sharing your ideas.

"Love Whispering. Do you think it will catch on?"

When people are ready, they will hear.

"Come on, let's head back to the hotel."

Now you're talking.

* * *

Lailah and I drift into a routine of surfing, walks along the beaches, massages at the spa and sunset dinners. It's a wonderful lifestyle, enough to keep anyone happy for a long, long time.

She introduces me to her friends and shows me her childhood hang-outs. We spend time splashing in the calm waters of Waikiki and touring the city shops and restaurants.

During the winter months the legendary North Shore beckons. Stretching for more than 11 kilometres, the beaches of the North Shore host the world's premier surfing competitions. November through February is the best time to watch big wave surfing. Neither Lailah nor I dare venture into the enormous winter waves, instead we opt to meander along beautiful Waimea Bay, Ehukai Beach (Banzai Pipeline) and Sunset Beach and leave the surfing to the professionals.

My radiant smile is hard to miss. *I love Oahu!*

"You do?"

What's not to love? You've got everything here. City living, warm climate, beaches, surfing.

"It was great growing up ..."

Something bothering you?

"Aren't you tired of living in hotels?"

Not really.

"I want to put down roots ... make a home."

We can do that here in Oahu.

"We have one more island to explore."

And then we decide where to settle?

"Yes."

Ah, we're about to move again.

"That was the deal."

You chartering a boat?

"As always."

How come we never fly?

She gives me an earnest look. "You don't have any documents. No identity, no passport."

Oh yeah.

"It would be very hard to explain who you are."

True.

Lailah wanders off to make a few phone calls. I can see she's a bit troubled. I hadn't really considered my unusual situation. It's an issue we will have to address at some point.

Half an hour later she announces the itinerary. We leave in the morning.

Time to hop north to Kauai.

* * *

The Garden Island has certainly earned its name. Kauai is dramatically beautiful, flaunting emerald valleys, jagged cliffs, cascading waterfalls and gorgeous beaches. It is the least populated of Hawaii's four counties (Kauai, Honolulu, Maui, Hawaii) with both development and tourism concentrated in relatively few locations. This has preserved the rich culture and laid-back atmosphere.

Lailah and I love it immediately.

"What does your heart tell you?"

This is it. A place to call home.

"I agree. And Oahu is nearby."

You in a hurry to settle down?

"Can we start house hunting soon?"

I smile. *Yep. No worries.*

Over the next few weeks we intersperse tours of the island with viewings of residential areas. We discover that it is generally warmer on the south and west sides, windier on the east side and rainier on the north shore. Kauai has more sand beaches along its 177-kilometre coastline than any other island and surfing opportunities abound. There are wonderful waves from Haena and Hanalei on the north shore to Kealia on the east shore, Poipu on the south shore and Polihale on the west shore.

We decide to purchase a house in Kaapa on the east coast. The town is situated mid-way between the north and south shores, giving us easy access to numerous surfing spots. Kapaa, which means 'solid' in Hawaiian, nestles at the base of Nounou (Sleeping Giant) Mountain and presents an array of hotels, shopping malls and restaurants. Everything we need is right here.

The single-storey house is situated in a quiet cul-de-sac. High ceilings, 4 bedrooms, 2.5 bathrooms, living room, dining room and detached garage. Wrap-around covered lanais provide a relaxing outdoor environment. The expansive lawn and tree-filled garden seal the deal. We make an offer and it is quickly accepted.

And so begins the next phase of our lives.

During breakfast one morning Lailah asks "Do you know what the term Aloha means?"

It seems to be used as a greeting, sometimes as a goodbye but mostly to say hello.

"Indeed. In the Hawaiian language it means 'affection, peace and compassion'. I think it's time to incorporate the spirit of Aloha into our lives."

What do you have in mind?

"The need to serve humanity is weaved into our essences."

True.

"Now that we are settled and free, let's connect with charitable foundations and offer our wealth, time and presence."

That is why I love you, you beautiful woman.

"Hope it's not the only reason."

I blow her a kiss. *One of countless …*

"Come have a look at these websites."

We amble to the flat screen and peruse the Hawaii Community Foundation, one of the oldest community foundations in the United States. The HCF is a public state-wide charitable services and grant-making organisation supported by donor contributions that invests in the people and communities of Hawaii. Next is the Hawaii Foodbank, a non-profit agency that collects, warehouses and distributes mass quantities of both perishable and non-perishable food throughout Hawaii so that 'no one in our family goes hungry'.

"Charity begins at home."

Absolutely. I would like to look further afield as well.

After a couple of hours I present my recommendations.

Lailah scans the website. 'World Vision is a humanitarian organisation dedicated to helping children, families and their communities reach their full potential by tackling the causes of poverty and injustice. Working in nearly 100 countries around the world, World Vision serves all people, regardless of religion, race, ethnicity or gender.'

"I like it."

And this one.

'WaterAid's vision is of a world where everyone has access to clean water, safe sanitation and good hygiene. Every minute, every day, people suffer and lives are lost needlessly because of a lack of safe water and sanitation. Help us end this global crisis and transform lives.'

"Wow, the statistics are frightening."

I know. We have to do something.

"Can we support all four charities? Two at home and two worldwide?"

It's the right thing to do. A fair balance.

"Aloha."

We set the wheels in motion. Soon our days are filled with charitable work, surfing and relaxing in our new home. Our lives remain uncomplicated and uncluttered. Neither of us cares much for possessions; consequently the house is sparsely furnished and our wardrobes contain just what we need.

It's a kind of Zen-like existence where the priority is not on *things,* rather on *people, heart-connection* and *experiences.* I believe this is how life is meant to be lived.

Now I am wondering about the next step. I have no birth certificate or identity document. Even the house had to be registered in her name.

How on earth do I propose to Lailah?

* * *

We are sitting on the beach at Kealia not far from home. Neither of us feels like surfing so it is an easy day ambling along the golden sand, splashing among the sapphire ripples and basking in the warm sun. The ocean air is marvellously revitalising.

I need some distraction from my document predicament.

Hey sweetheart …

"Hmm?"

Care to share more of your Love Whispering ideas?

"Are you sure?"

Yep.

She takes a deep breath. "Remember our last discussion? The single greatest challenge facing most relationships is communication. Males and females usually have very different perception and communication styles."

I nod.

"On top of that, most people have mediocre listening skills."

I'm sorry. What were you saying?

She playfully smacks my arm.

"The majority of conversations between people take the form of back-and-forth dialogue or banter. This is completely natural and ideal for social bonding and information exchange."

Mmm ... that's how most people speak with each other.

"However, we need to reserve a place for Egoless Listening. Here attention is focused solely on the other person, a technique quite rare in most societies."

Why would you use egoless listening?

"This type of listening is about experiencing and building a deeper connection. It's like a gift you give at special times. Although you can use it socially and professionally, it is ideally used in your intimate relationships. It creates a feeling of being truly heard, recognised and loved."

Is it a passive form of listening? Where you say and do nothing?

"Just the opposite. A silent stoical stare does not create a listening ambience. Egoless listening employs a number of active techniques."

Aha.

"First you need to remove all distractions and completely focus on the other person. Put your own thoughts, agendas and stories aside. This is not about you, and you will not be sharing your mind."

Empty of self.

"You must show your interest by using open body language – eye contact, nodding, uncrossed arms – and verbal encouragement: 'tell me more', 'mmm …'"

I quietly unfold my arms.

"After you have those basic techniques in place, you can start to employ the more advanced techniques. It is important that you do everything in a natural manner."

Tell me more.

"Technique 1: Reflect The Facts. This simply means that you repeat back in your own words what your partner has said. Use phrases like 'If I heard you correctly, you are saying …'; 'If I understand you, you mean …'; 'In other words, you're saying …'"

You mean I should paraphrase in order to check my understanding?

"Correct."

She pauses and watches a nonchalant surfer carving a white-tipped wave.

"Technique 2: Reflect The Emotion. Here you mention the emotion as well as the facts. Use phrases like 'I get the sense you're sad ...'; 'I hear anxiety in your voice ...'; 'It sounds like you are delighted about the results ...'"

You seem relaxed and happy when you share your ideas.

"Technique 3: Use The Echo. Take the main word or phrase and repeat it as a question."

As a question?

She smiles and nods.

"Technique 4: Summarise. Offer a condensed version of what you have heard."

Egoless listening is about focusing actively and exclusively on the other person. It differs from the day to day casual dialogue and banter. It deepens the connection and creates a feeling of being recognised and loved. We can use any number of techniques, including reflection, echoing and summarising.

"Wow, nice job! My work here is done."

I realise that egoless listening cannot be a bland technique. It is essential to infuse the responses with unconditional love and acceptance.

"Indeed. Energy follows intention."

Could you sense the flow of loving energy?

"Of course."

Love is the secret ingredient of effective communication.

"Love Whispering is the secret ingredient of joyful relationships."

Thank you for sharing those wonderful ideas.

"You're welcome, my darling."

I throw my arms back and stare into the azure sky. For a brief moment a familiar green, silver and gold plumage flits across my vision. Then it disappears.

The hummingbird in my dream.

* * *

Lailah and I are cruising around the island. Our first port of call is Hanapepe Town, a rustic plantation-style south shore village filled with fine art galleries displaying paintings, handmade ceramics, glassware and rare koa woodwork. Every Friday from 6-9pm painters, sculptors and craftspeople throw open the doors of their galleries and studios in a celebration called Art Night.

After a relaxed viewing we purchase a large painting of the Banzai Pipeline, a surf reef break located off Ehukai Beach Park at Oahu's North Shore. Pipeline, as it is informally known, is famous for huge waves breaking in shallow water just above a sharp reef, forming the hallowed cylindrical tubes that provide surfing nirvana.

Over dinner we gaze at our awe-inspiring memento, at once a sweet reminder of Lailah's childhood home and glorious emblem of our passion for the ocean and surfing.

The next day we drive to Waimea Canyon on Kauai's west side, sometimes described as the Grand Canyon of the Pacific. The first good vantage point is Waimea Canyon Lookout, offering panoramic views of crested buttes, rugged crags and deep valley gorges. 23 kilometres long, 1.6 kilometres wide and over 1 kilometre deep, it is an impressive sight.

The road continues into the mountains and ends at Kokee State Park, a vast spread of rainforest luxuriating in a cool wet climate. We wander along a trail and delight in the diverse plant life, ranging from the native Mokihana berry (the official flower of Kauai) to the imported Australian eucalyptus and Californian redwood. The finishing touch is Kalalau Lookout where we savour a breathtaking vista across the magenta cliffs.

Tonight we are staying at the Waimea Plantation Cottages, a cluster of carefully restored historic cottages nestled amid a peaceful coconut grove on the west coast. Located at the seaside, with period-inspired furniture and modern conveniences, it is the perfect place to spend the rest of the weekend.

As we are drifting into sleep I turn Lailah onto her tummy and place my arm across her back. She always feels really loved in this position. My heart feels warm as I whisper into her ear *I love sharing my life with you.*

She mumbles "Love you too" then the night captures us.

* * *

We're home. Another Monday of mowing the lawn and doing the grocery shopping. The simple routines that comprise a shared life. The sun is beaming upon my shoulders while a soft breeze ruffles my hair.

Lailah is tending to the flower beds. I look across at her and smile.

I'm not in the mood for work today. I feel kinda lazy ...

"Me neither."

Let's go for a drive and get lost in nature.

"What about the Wailua River? It's just down the road."

Good idea. I'll pack some cold drinks and snacks.

Flowing from Mount Waialeale in the centre of the island and 32 kilometres long, it is one of the only navigable rivers in Hawaii. Soon we are parked at the roadside watching the tranquil Opaekaa Falls. From here we traipse across to the gorgeous Wailua Falls to appreciate its cascading 52-metre streams.

The padded picnic blanket spreads cosily over the lush greenery. We pin the corners with the cooler box and sandals then stretch out and enjoy the surroundings.

I touch her hand and sigh. *We live in an amazing place.*

"That we do."

It is quiet for a long while, then "Are you ready for more Love Whispering?"

Yeah, why not. It all helps the relationship.

"Here come the advanced teachings. You need to fasten your seatbelt."

I'm ready.

Lailah reaches for a twig then draws a triangle in the soft soil. "I call this the Love Triangle."

Cute.

At the apex she writes the word Matching.

"The starting point for every romantic relationship is finding a good match. Even though this seems obvious it is surprising how few people understand its importance. This is partly because distracting myths abound and partly because we get sidetracked by sexual and physical attraction."

What kind of myths?

"The most common one is that 'opposites attract'. This directly contradicts the research findings of relationship psychology and life experience."

What is the truth?

"Similarities Attract. Finding someone similar to you strongly increases your chances of having a fulfilling and long-lasting relationship. Small differences may create a pleasant tension but if there is too much disparity the relationship usually ends in heartache. Therefore you need to ensure a range of commonalities in a prospective romantic partner.

"The Equity Principle also comes into play. When you meet someone you tend to unconsciously assess if they are equal to you – physically, mentally, emotionally, socially, professionally. You are trying to assess if it will be a fair trade."

Sounds so romantic.

"It is unromantic to ignore those principles. And destructive."

Ouch.

"Another myth is the idea of Mr or Ms Perfect. Perfection does not exist and it's a long lonely wait. You need to look for someone who is a good match then practice the techniques of Love Whispering."

What you see is what you get.

"Ooh, can I borrow that?"

Yep.

"It leads nicely to the next principle: Never fall in love with someone's potential. They are either a good match or not. People seldom change, no matter how much you love them. What you see is what you get."

In summary: Seek someone who has similar values, beliefs, passions and interests. Allow a few differences. Accept that person just as they are. Diligently practise the communication and listening skills.

"Voila!"

Now, where to find such a person ... considering the low odds of meeting an angel.

"It makes sense to search for a romantic partner at places that you enjoy visiting. For example, spiritual events and social activities that give you pleasure. You are looking for someone with similar interests to you."

Good strategy.

Lailah hands me the twig. "At the bottom left point of the Love Triangle write the word Needs."

Ok.

"This is the second crucial concept. Once you have found a good match, you need to learn about your partner's needs."

Seems straightforward.

"On the contrary, this is fraught with confusion and difficulties."

In what way?

"Society, culture and the media have taught us to ignore our innermost needs. Acknowledging needs is generally seen as weak. Ever heard the phrase 'You're so needy'? It is often spoken with disdain, as if there is something unnatural about having needs. We are also told that it is selfish to express our needs. Consequently, we learn to skilfully repress our needs and eventually lose the ability to discern our needs."

How sad.

"The truth is we all have needs. As long as you are alive in this body you have needs. Psychological and emotional needs are no less important than physical needs. Love and affection are as necessary as food and water."

So the first step is acknowledging that you have needs.

"True. Some of your needs are met by work, friends, family and recreational interests. Others are only met through a romantic relationship."

Romantic partners ideally fulfil each other's intimate needs.

"One of the greatest secrets to a satisfying relationship is discovering what your partner needs, then striving to fulfil those needs. This is neither a selfish love that focuses entirely on you nor a selfless love that focuses entirely on your partner. The intention is not to slave over each other or constantly try to please each other."

It should be a mutually beneficial relationship with reciprocal loving-kindness.

"Nice. You're going to put me out of a job."

The next step is discovering each other's needs.

117

"Most people are completely out of practice. It is essential that you take the time to access your own needs, then have the courage to share those needs with your partner. There is no other way forward."

In summary: Ignore what you have been taught by society, culture and the media. Accept that humans have psychological, emotional and physical needs. Ponder your own needs. Express them openly to your partner. Listen to your partner's needs. Practise fulfilling each other's needs.

"The key is to risk sharing your specific needs. What exactly do you want? This is no time to be vague or circumspect. The life of your romantic relationship depends on full disclosure."

I can imagine some people still trying to guess what their partner requires. Or copiously giving their partner what they believe is required, instead of what their partner truly wants. Frustrating, disappointing and exhausting for both parties.

"Exactly. Your partner is not psychic. It is not their job to 'automatically know your needs because they love you'. That is ludicrous. You need to tell them."

Many people are quite clear about what they don't want in a relationship.

"Tell me what you want, not what you don't want."

Well spoken.

"Romantic partnerships thrive on need fulfilment. However, without detailed disclosure of needs even the most well matched relationship will fade away and finish."

That's worth remembering.

"Introspection and courageous conversation will be necessary. You need to create your own Need Map and share it with your partner. You also need to discover your partner's Need Map."

Need Map?

"The list of your specific and detailed needs under the following headings: Security, Friendship, Affection, Attention, Appreciation, Sex."

Excellent idea.

"The secret is to do it, not speculate about it. Your romantic relationship, like all your relationships, is at least partly your responsibility. If you want to experience deep and lasting fulfilment, you have to take action."

Strategic action realises your dreams.

"Keep in mind that even with the best intentions you will sometimes fall back into your old ways and re-enact previous mistakes. When that happens, be kind. Forgive yourself and your partner quickly. The secret is determination and persistence."

Wow. I feel motivated!

Lailah takes a deep breath, sighs and collapses onto the blanket. I lean over and kiss her face softly, my fingertips ruffling her hair and gently massaging her scalp. She purrs contentedly.

After fifteen minutes I ask the inevitable question. *What about the third point on the triangle?*

She rolls over onto her elbows. "Are you sure you can handle it? There's been a lot to digest."

Are you kidding? You can't leave me wondering.

I position the twig in my hand and wait expectantly.

"Ok. At the bottom right point, write the word Magic."

Ah, sounds interesting.

"So ... you've found a good match and worked hard to discover, express and fulfil each other's needs. The relationship should now be secure and satisfying."

I wink. *Oh, it is baby.*

"Your goal is to compile a Magic List. This goes beyond fulfilling needs. It takes your relationship a step further, adding the icing to the cake. You are now dreaming up romantic, fun and significant things to give to your partner and do for your partner."

Awesome.

"Unlike the Need Map which is discussed explicitly and openly with your partner, the Magic List is collated gradually and in secret. You will never share this information with your partner. However, the same rules apply: Give your partner what they want, not what you think they want; focus on significant things not grand gestures or expensive gifts; focus on quality not quantity."

How can you collect this information?

"Quietly observe your partner. Think about their hobbies, interests and dreams. Listen to comments they make when watching television or reading a magazine. Talk surreptitiously to their friends and family."

Hmm ...

She sits up and stretches her arms high. "And that, my friend, is that. The core of Love Whispering. A triangle comprising Matching, Needs and Magic."

I love it. Insightful and full of wisdom.

"Yet without action it comes to nothing."

True.

I open the cooler box and unpack a small bottle of champagne, two flutes and a punnet of strawberries. She beams a huge smile. An unsurprising response ... I've been making a few notes of my own.

We raise our glasses and clink them happily.

To many years of love and magic.

"Love and magic."

* * *

Taking on a human form has clearly highlighted the importance of Love Whispering. No matter how spiritual you are, no matter where you originate, no matter how awake you may be, the fact is you need intelligent and pragmatic techniques to create effective and fulfilling relationships.

And I am not finding it too hard. The secret is to commit to a new strategy. To dedicate yourself to beneficial behaviours. Fortunately Lailah and I are moving in the same direction. If only one partner is doing the work, it becomes far more challenging, requiring vast amounts of patience, perseverance and forgiveness.

What did that surfing instructor tell me? 'The only way you achieve anything is with knowledge, tutorship and practice, practice, practice.' As with any new skill, you fall off the board many times but you get up and keep trying. Then one day it just starts to flow ...

I have noticed that it is easier to work on the Magic List than the Need Map. Sometimes my mind wrestles with my heart and I am unable to identify my feelings and needs.

One morning I ask Lailah about this matter.

She fetches a book from the study and hands it to me. "It's called Nonviolent Communication: A Language of Life. The author is Marshall Rosenberg. It is absolutely the best book about relationships. You should read it."

I will. Can you give me some thought-starters?

"According to Nonviolent Communication, three primary questions are vital when it comes to relationships:

"What am I feeling, needing and requesting?

"What is the other feeling, needing and requesting?

"What can be done to make our lives more wonderful?"

Interesting.

"The idea is to get away from destructive behaviours like criticism, blaming, dredging up the past, scorecarding, diagnosing, judging, moralising, insulting and labelling. Instead we learn to listen deeply to ourselves and others, so that we can identify and express needs. This is a natural and healthy approach to relationships."

Most people are excellent at complaining and criticising.

"Those destructive behaviours are comparable to death by a thousand cuts. A guaranteed way to gradually wound and devastate a relationship."

I wonder how many people are adept at accessing their feelings and needs.

"It is definitely a skill which most people have forgotten or never learned. It can be even tougher learning to express those feelings and needs."

Lailah pulls a little note out of her purse. On it reads:

I feel
I need
I request
I let go

That's awesome. A great reminder.

"Seriously, you need to read this book. Then lock the principles in your mind and practise, practise, practise. It's the master class on attaining peace and fulfilment in social and romantic relationships."

My fingers slowly trace the bright yellow sunflower on the cover. Then I walk to the living room, drop into my favourite recliner chair, turn to the first page and begin reading.

It's time to take our relationship to the next joyful level.

* * *

Lailah and I are strapping the boards to the soft roof racks on our van. Our passion for surfing necessitated a bit of investment – a spacious vehicle modified to allow dining and sleeping. It's super-comfy and has a great sound system.

Poipu on the south shore is only an hour away and The Beach Boys blaring through the speakers will keep us in good spirits.

We arrive to a perfect day. Cloudless sapphire sky, flowing wave sets, soft breeze. Our toes crunch in the sand as we amble down to feel the water.

Oh yeah. It's all rock 'n roll.

"A quick snack and I'm ready."

What are you going to eat?

"Fruit salad and raisins."

Light energy boost. Good move.

We run to the van and open the cooler box. I find the container then make a wild face and shout *Snack attack!*

Lailah bursts into laughter. "You silly man. Give me that."

Soon we are happily munching and watching the surf.

I'm fired up. It's going to be a great day.

"That's for sure."

Do you feel that serene energy? A kind of spiritual ambience.

"Angel."

Huh?

"Messenger."

Really? How do you know?

She shrugs. "I've always known. It's how I knew you were hanging around me."

Give me some clues.

"It's that pleasant shiver along the spine. That moment of unusual peace and clarity. The sense of a light shining in the background."

Oh yeah. I get that now.

"Guardians are always present so you get used to the energy and barely notice it. Messengers are different – they tend to come and go – so you notice the variance in energy. And they have unique energy signatures."

How do you know all this?

"I've been sensing you angels for a long time. Intuiting your ways. The visit to your world confirmed my beliefs and understanding."

Impressive.

"The Messenger must be here for a reason. They don't hang around like Guardians."

I can't see them. Let's surf.

"Yeah. No point waiting."

I am already wearing my surf shorts; just need a rash vest. Lailah slips into her bikini. We grab the boards and run into the water.

The waves surge exhilaration through our bodies. We paddle out beyond the break and survey the incoming swell.

Whoo hoo! Here we go …

"See you later …"

She's off ... no doubt elegantly carving and snapping a marvellous roller. I catch the face of the next wave and chase after her.

Three hours later we are laying on the warm sand laughing at some inane joke. We move into the shade and unpack the sweet breads, salad and fruit juice. Time for a light lunch and well deserved rest.

Then we pummel the water again, duck-diving our way to the back line. This time I snatch the first wave. It's a beauty. I run my fingers along the curling water and glide horizontally along the face. Suddenly the energy becomes fabulously serene. A deep stillness engulfs me.

Green-silver-gold blurs across my vision. Thrown off balance, I crash into the churning water and tumble toward the shore. Arriving in the shallows, I pull my board close, take a few deep breaths and look for her.

A glint of sunlight catches my attention. Floating a couple of metres from me is a bottle. It irks me immediately; I cannot stand the litter that floods our oceans. I wade across to retrieve it then walk to the beach.

Lailah joins me a few minutes later.

"What are you doing? You alright?"

Found this bottle and couldn't leave it out there.

She squints her eyes. "What's inside?"

Hmm? I don't know.

"Is that a message in a bottle? Open it."

I remove the cork and a tightly rolled document slides out.

She sits next to me. "What is it?"

A deft unfurling reveals a birth certificate: Michael Walker, male, born in Kauai.

Is that real?

"I'm no expert but it looks exactly like my Hawaiian birth certificate."

This must be a hoax.

"There's the official stamp. Check the birth date: Michael is 28 years old."

Quietness settles upon us. Is the ocean swoosh trying to tell us the answer? I gather some sand and sprinkle it slowly over my toes.

I think I saw the hummingbird during my last ride.

"There are no coincidences. I'm sure it's genuine."

We can get it officially verified.

She smiles. "Welcome to planet earth, Mr Walker."

* * *

The next few weeks are a frenzy of officialdom and paperwork interspersed among our regular work with humanitarian organisations.

It is not long before I am declared a Hawaiian citizen. Soon I have my passport and the house is transferred into joint ownership. Now we can truly begin to settle into our new life.

Lailah has never looked happier.

I surreptitiously seek a jeweller who can create the engagement ring of her dreams. 'White gold with a mounted pearl – from my necklace' as I recall. We choose a cream South Sea pearl as it will harmonise gorgeously with her ring.

Time to put the next stage of my cunning plan into operation. Should it be an engagement party or a private affair ... or both? I still don't have any friends – something to work on – but Lailah has a few on Oahu. Contacting her friends will allow me to garner ideas for a romantic event.

I hire a wedding company to organise the special occasion. The location will be the Banzai Pipeline on Oahu's North Shore, making our painting even more significant. It will start with just the two of us then move to a small gathering further down the beach. A week night seems best so we can avoid the crowds.

For a being who has spent its life living with openness and transparency, it is rather difficult engaging in deception. I have to keep reminding myself of the higher purpose. Hopefully she does not suspect anything.

We fly to Oahu and book into a hotel on the North Shore, under the guise of a four-day getaway. On the Tuesday evening I suggest a barefoot stroll on Ehukai Beach, with the hint of a romantic dinner. It is an hour before sunset, plenty of time to allow everything to fall into place.

Our casual chat mysteriously turns to the subject of marriage.

I've been thinking ...

"Hmm?"

I shrug nonchalantly. *I have an identity now, official papers.*

"You do."

Do you ever think about the future?

She looks at me suspiciously. "Meaning?"

We are interrupted by a woman selling leis.

"Wow, those are beautiful."

I nod at the vendor. *We'll take two.*

She carefully drapes garlands of flowers around our necks.

"Mmm, wonderful scent."

We saunter along the rippling sand. A sapphire wave breaks in the distance.

I was wondering ...

"What is it, my darling?"

How would you feel about spending the rest of your life with me?

"That's the plan."

I drop to one knee and open the blue velvet box.

Lailah, will you marry me?

Her hands swiftly cover her mouth as her eyes widen with shock and joy.

"Of course I'll marry you!"

I gently place the ring on her finger. She moves her hand closer and inspects it.

"Oh Michael, it's perfect."

Nothing will give me greater joy than sharing my life with you.

"Marrying you has always been my dream."

The kiss is passionate and tender.

I love you, sweetheart.

"I love you too."

Come this way. I want to show you something.

We amble along the beach until we see tall white candles lighting a flower-petal pathway. Hawaiian singers croon soft melodies as we approach. Her friends are waiting at a white-clothed dinner table. They rush over to dispense hearty congratulations and scrutinise the ring. Lailah is in tears.

The waiter serves flutes of champagne and we make a toast.

To love and friendship.

"Love and friendship."

The timing could not be better. The sun is setting and the heavens are glowing pink and gold. It's going to a spectacular evening.

* * *

My eyes flutter open. A week has passed since our engagement. It's wonderful to be home in Kauai.

"Hey fiancé ..."

Hey beautiful.

"Can I wake up next to you for the rest of my life?"

Please do.

Her hair is sprinkled across the white pillow. I am under the spell of the lover's gaze. There is something quite magical when two people truly see each other. Unguarded eyes, undefended energy, surrendered into what is and whatever shall be.

This exquisite union of the hearts … I think it is what we are all seeking. Perhaps love in all its forms is the one true antidote to the strange, struggling emptiness of existence.

On a very real and basic level, there is terrible hardship for so many people on this planet. A lack of essential survival resources. Poverty and starvation and disease. Moving up a level, we have those with enough to survive but limited access to a better quality of life. Then there are people with good jobs but who somehow feel unhappy and unfulfilled.

I recall seeing these statistics in one of Lailah's academic journals: In Western societies (USA and Europe) the average age of onset for depressive disorders fifty years ago was 29 years old; today the average age of onset is 15 years old. Also, approximately 10% of the population aged 18 and older suffer from a depressive disorder in any given year.

What does that tell you?

Why do societies, governments and corporations allow fellow humans to suffer? Why are societies watching the destruction of forests and oceans with such nonchalance? How do governments justify so badly polluting an atmosphere that citizens are forced to wear filter-masks? How do shareholders and corporations get away with siphoning the wealth and resources of our planet into their deep pockets?

This world is broken and no one seems ready to admit it.

"Hello. Where are you?"

Just thinking about a few things.

"Care to share?"

The state of our planet. It really bothers me.

"Tell me more."

We are giving so much. Trying to make a difference.

"Uh huh."

Why are people homeless? Why doesn't every person have a job? Why aren't we guaranteeing a minimum state of dignity for each individual?

"I hear that."

If we take care of our brothers and sisters, does that mean we have to surrender innovation, development and progress on our planet? Are the poor perceived to be a drain on available capital? Surely everyone deserves a minimum standard of living? Surely everyone wants to work toward common goals like global health and prosperity?

"There has to be a way."

It's the systems that need to change, not the people. We need to guarantee every individual access to water, food, sanitation, shelter and education. There has to be a minimum bottom rung on this planet. Beyond that, people are free to pursue achievement and excellence as they choose.

"Are you wanting to end capitalism?"

I have no interest in stifling progress. Equally I cannot endure the suffering of fellow humans. We need to rein in this obscene exploitation and create a system of responsible capitalism and entrepreneurship.

"Wow, that's a lot to do before breakfast."

I force a smile. Being trapped in an earth body makes confrontation with earth truths inevitable.

Alright, let's get something to eat. I'm hungry.

"A bowl of granola sprinkled with goji berries?"

Mmm …

"You feel like driving to the north shore this weekend?"

Catch a few waves?

"Yes, and maybe stay overnight."

Let's do it.

We finish our charitable work for the week and load the van on the Friday afternoon. Jack Johnson is mellowing the speakers as we cruise along the coastal Kuhio Highway.

"Love this music …"

This is our song.

"Better Together?"

Yep … it's always better when we're together …

Soon we are singing the lyrics in happy unison.

We arrive in Haena. White fluffy clouds are churning the sky. Intermittent sunrays are peeking through the cotton blanket and making the trees glimmer. A cool wind is blowing.

Lailah shivers. "I don't mind sleeping in the van but let's eat out tonight."

Any ideas?

"The Mediterranean Gourmet. It's won a few best restaurant awards. The menu is a fusion of Lebanese, French, Spanish, Italian and Greek influences."

I'm in.

We stare at the crashing waves for a while then make our way to the restaurant. The waiter seats us by the window. We savour the pleasant ambience, panoramic ocean view and delicious food. As the evening drifts by, I marvel at the woman across the table. She's mine and I'm hers. We belong together and it's a wonderful feeling.

After dinner we park the van, open the sunroof and lay on our bed. The weather has cleared. Holding her in my arms, I stare at the stars. A sudden déjà vu grips my consciousness ... we've done this before ... on an island somewhere ... a warm feeling infuses my being ... serenity overcomes me and I gradually fade away ...

* * *

In the morning we drive to Hanalei Bay. It is the largest bay on the island, comprising 3 kilometres of sandy beach bordered by the Waipa River to the west and the Hanalei River to the east.

We sit and watch the cobalt-blue ocean rolling before us. At one end of the beach is a 91-metre pier used for fishing and swimming. The bay is set against a serene backdrop of waterfalls and emerald mountain peaks. It's a stunning location.

A quick change and we plunge into the water.

It's amazing how the hours disappear when you are carving waves. Exhilarating, peaceful and connected to the raw power of nature, surfing offers the complete physical and spiritual experience.

At midday we find some shade under the trees, spread out the picnic blanket and open the cooler box. Fruit juice and sandwiches and chill time. Just what we need.

"Wow, do you feel that?"

Huh?

"That energy. It's familiar."

Oh yeah. Messenger?

"Nope."

You're amazingly sensitive.

"You're not trying."

I put down my sandwich. *Hmm … felt that before …*

"What is it?"

I remember tumbling off my board.

"The hummingbird."

Yep.

"The presence is strong."

Luminous green-silver-gold plumage flits into view. A brilliant hummingbird is hovering before us.

Salutations.

"Avatar."

How's the antidote coming along?

The tiny dark eyes seem to penetrate my essence.

Antidote?

You said 'Love in all its forms is the one true antidote for the strange, struggling emptiness of existence.'

Ah yes, I did.

Um ... Lailah and I love each other deeply. We are doing lots of charitable work.

Still staring at me.

It's just the madness of life on this planet. The suffering on every level. And the not knowing.

The gaze does not abate.

Every person will die. And their stories will fade and disappear. And then what was it all for?

Relentless flapping.

The futile search for meaning. Scrutinising a blank canvas and expecting an answer.

I look at Lailah and shrug helplessly.

Everything quietens. The swift-moving wings make no sound. It's almost unbearable.

Life is a series of stories that you create in order to learn about Love. Your job is to immerse yourself in each story but not attach to it.

"Why?"

The gaze locks onto Lailah. I sigh with relief.

Love is the energy surrounding the Light.

"And the Light is our ultimate destination?"

You are the Light and you are discovering yourself.

A puzzle wrapped in an enigma. Nice.

"Ok, can we backtrack a little?"

Nothing.

"From a separated perspective, we are individual points of consciousness journeying back to the Source."

Stillness.

"The field of energy surrounding the Source is Love. So we have to become Love before fully entering and becoming one with the Light, before merging with the Source."

Quietness.

You can experience glimpses of the Source; you can swim in the Light; but you will never fully return until you can harmonise with and move through the energy of Love.

"Ah, I get it."

Aren't you breaking the rules by conversing with us?

"Avatars work outside the systems."

What do you mean?

"Avatars are the rebels of the universe. Powerful beings that interfere in various systems. They are not limited by rules."

How do you know all this?

"Your memories are blocked. When I visited your world, we spoke with the hummingbird."

Who are you? My voice is so strong it startles me.

Light of the highest order, agitating systems to the next level.

A catalyst?

Indeed.

The serene stillness envelops us once more. Our peaceful altered state of consciousness is softly massaged by the ocean swoosh.

Eventually Lailah speaks. "Can you tell us more about the function of the Messengers?"

Teachers and guides. Bound to the Three Immutable Laws.

I whisper to her. *Remind me again?*

"You may not reveal yourself. You may not interfere with free will. You may not interrupt the flow of Life."

Ah.

She directs her attention to the hummingbird. "How do they guide us without breaking the laws?"

You sense their presence, yet they are not revealing themselves. They flow encouragement into your energy field, yet they are not interfering. They whisper beneficial hints, yet they do not interrupt the flow of Life.

"Is that why fallen angels lose their memories?"

My ears prick up immediately.

Of course.

"To ensure compliance with the laws."

Memories are blocked but energy is unaltered.

"I don't understand."

You cannot change the essence of a being. Angelic vibrations will trickle into every aspect of their life.

"So fallen angels will tend to work with philanthropic organisations and humanitarian movements. Have little interest in acquiring possessions or accumulating wealth. Be naturally altruistic. And attract deeply spiritual and loving partners."

Exactly. Except for the last one.

"Oh?"

Sometimes they choose to walk alone.

"Can the angelic essence leak into the human mind?"

Yes. Manifesting in the form of flashbacks, déjà vu and inexplicable inner knowing.

I nod silently. Good to know.

"Can any angel decide to fall?"

Every being in the universe has free will. Considering the sacrifice of falling, an angel will do it only for a higher purpose.

"You mean like a mission?"

For Love. In all its forms.

It becomes quiet again. The cogs are clearly turning in Lailah's mind.

"Are Walkers fulfilling a higher purpose?"

The angelic essence in you automatically raises the vibration of the human souls around you. Plus the type of work you do usually benefits the planet.

"God's secret agents ..."

Walkers generally appear as ordinary humans living ordinary lives. A few incarnate to bring social and political change. Many work for humanitarian organisations.

"Mother Teresa? Mahatma Gandhi? Nelson Mandela?"

What is known and what is not known.

And with that obscure sign-off the hummingbird disappears, leaving us much to ponder and discuss.

We spend the rest of the day ambling along the beach, frolicking in the shallow water and mulling over the sacrosanct words.

* * *

The next morning we are woken by driving rain. Dark clouds everywhere. Not sure how long this storm will last.

Lailah yawns and stretches. "We need a hotel for tonight."

I'm with you.

We cruise around Hanalei and find a place to stay. The warm shower is refreshing and soon I feel like a new person. A hot breakfast gets us ready for the day.

Refusing to be held captive by the weather we drive across to the island's northernmost point: Kilauea Lighthouse. A glimmer of sunlight invites us to jump out and savour the spectacular view of rugged coastline and deep blue ocean. This is also the home of the Kilauea Point National Wildlife Refuge, a sanctuary for seabirds, and a great spot for whale watching.

We visit the colourful shops and galleries in Hanalei Town, then as the sky clears we drop by the verdant Limahuli Tropical Botanical Gardens which are nestled beneath Makana Mountain.

Finally we settle at Kee Beach. The sun is beaming brightly so I throw a blanket on the warm sand and open the cooler box.

Snack attack?

"Yes please."

Fruit salad?

"Mmm, that'll do."

I unwrap one of the fresh sandwiches made by the hotel.

Cold drink? Still or sparkling water?

"Sparkling."

Soon we are savouring our late lunch and enjoying the gorgeous weather.

"Yesterday flustered my mind."

I nod. *It's a lot to contemplate.*

"Do you realise that we are surrounded by angels?"

I take another bite of the delicious sandwich.

"Each one of us has a Guardian. And the Messengers regularly come and go."

Indeed.

"On top of that, who knows how many angels have fallen and walk among us."

They walk among us.

She strokes her arm thoughtfully. "Yep ... like air-beings."

Huh?

"Invisible and everywhere ... as if in the air around us."

Ok.

"So many subtle and hidden influences."

I guess we are not alone after all.

"That's for sure."

How does that change anything? We still have to make choices and live our lives.

"I think you summed it up already: We are not alone."

My toes reach across the blanket and brush the soft sand.

I guess our journey is inescapable.

"Meaning?"

We are creating our reality. We are choosing our adventures.

"Uh huh."

And we will continue until we blend with Love then enter the Light.

"Yes."

The speed of the journey is up to us. For some, the slow circuitous route. For others, a direct path.

"I know where I want to go when this body dies."

My home world?

She nods. "I call it heaven."

A sudden shearing of my consciousness. This conversation is familiar.

There are infinite realities and some souls aspire to explore other dimensions.

She looks at me strangely. "And I say 'Are some realities closer to the Source?'"

There are many realities on the way to the Source. You choose your own journey. It all depends on what you seek, what you desire.

"Your world is very close to the Source, isn't it?"

Yes, Lailah, it is.

I clasp my head tightly in my hands. My body is trembling.

What just happened? Was that a déjà vu?

"Yep, we exchanged those exact words in the Maldives."

Wow. The angel essence is leaking into my mind.

"It's wonderful."

I jump to my feet. *Come on, I'll race you to the water.*

We splash playfully then go for a long swim. The rippling waves wash over my body and the confusion subsides. I may not know all the answers, but I do know one thing: For me, heaven is being with this woman.

At the end of the day we make the hour-long drive home. It's been quite a weekend and I am looking forward to the predictable routine.

* * *

We are immersed in our charity projects. It seems we have little time for ourselves at the moment. Lailah is on an international assignment and I am island hopping to garner support for a new humanitarian programme. She has only been gone a few days and I miss her terribly.

I can't imagine what it would be like living without her.

Pushing that gloomy thought from my mind, I focus on the task at hand. A presentation to a number of wealthy businessmen. Remember the key phrases: 'corporate social responsibility' … 'investing in people and planet' … 'leave something beautiful for your children' … 'the Native Hawaiian concept of malama aina or caring for the land' … 'together we can make a difference'.

It takes two weeks to secure the funding. We are going to have to hire new people. Our charitable organisation is expanding faster than anticipated.

Tears well when she arrives at the airport. We kiss and melt into each other's arms.

"Missed you so much."

Me too.

"This 'spaces in your togetherness' thing is overrated."

Too much space, not enough togetherness.

"Did you water the plants?"

What plants?

She slaps my arm. "I love those plants."

Not more than me, I hope.

"Tell me."

Of course I did.

"Take me home."

At your service, Ma'am.

She smiles and reaches for my hand.

During the drive back I notice her eyes are closing. Long flights can be exhausting.

I haul the suitcase indoors and we sprawl on the sofa.

"Is there anything light to eat?"

Some chicken soup? They say it's good for the soul.

"Thank you. It's about all I can manage."

We dine quietly together then trudge to the bedroom. I am ready to make love all night but she won't last another ten minutes.

I tuck her in and kiss her forehead. The last thing I hear is a muffled "I love you". A little snore, a body tremor and she's asleep.

In the morning I make her favourite breakfast and place it on a tray. A budding red rose in a slim vase completes the arrangement.

The wafting aromas rouse her. "Hey …"

Hey beautiful.

"Is that for me?"

I nod.

"Give me a minute."

She bounds out the bedroom and disappears. I take the opportunity to reposition her pillows.

"This is for you, my darling."

A gift?

"Yep."

Lailah settles into her breakfast while I rip the maroon paper. In the box is a small crystal statue. I extract it and hold it up to the light. It's an iridescent hummingbird.

"You like it?"

Mmm ... exquisite.

I spin it around, watching how beautifully it refracts the sunrays.

"Maybe it will release some memories."

I shall have to find a special place for it.

"Perhaps on a window ledge."

I'm going to name it.

"Really? What?"

That darn hummingbird.

"Wow, it's working already."

Hmm?

"Never mind."

So tell me about your trip.

We spend the next hour sharing our experiences and swapping ideas for the charitable projects.

It's the end of a long fortnight. I look at her and smile. *Today is our day. Our weekend starts now.*

"Do you feel like walking along Kealia beach later?"

That would be lovely. First we have some catching up to do.

She pulls back the cover and invites me in.

I grin happily. *It's good to have you home.*

"It's good to be home."

* * *

Kealia has strong currents and wind swell but offers reasonably consistent surf. We decide to take the boards. It will be great to feel the water cascading over us again.

We leave our sandals in the van and stroll along the glistening sand. Lailah seems quiet and thoughtful. I ask if something is bothering her.

She stands still for a moment and gazes at a swaying palm. "I had plenty of time to consider the teachings of the hummingbird."

I'm listening.

"You know I receive glimpses of my missing years?"

Yep. Never about your earthly childhood though.

"Exactly. Strange memories of travelling through space, and soaring among the stars, and visiting different planets."

You wondered if it was just your imagination.

"I know. But the hummingbird spoke about flashbacks and inexplicable inner knowing."

True ...

"At the north shore, I asked if Walkers are fulfilling a higher purpose."

Uh huh.

"The hummingbird was looking directly at me when it said 'The angelic essence in you automatically raises the vibration of the human souls around you.'"

I cast my mind back to the event. *Hmm ... that's right.*

"What if we are both fallen angels? That may explain why we get on so well together."

Wow. That's radical.

"My essence is leaking into my human mind too. Those memories are real."

I sit down on the warm sand. Is it possible? Is Lailah an angel?

Wait a minute. I was your Guardian. Wouldn't I have known?

"How many angels are there? Did you know all of them?"

Probably not.

"Before you fell, you explained the angelic hierarchy to me. You never knew about Walkers."

I didn't?

"No. Apparently that information was beyond your level."

I thought my world was open and transparent.

"More déjà vu ..."

Huh?

"This is weird. What's going on here?"

What do you mean?

"It feels like we are moving along a pre-planned route."

Who's doing the planning?

"The hummingbird would say it's us."

Ok, now I'm confused.

"What was the teaching about stories?"

Life is a series of stories that you create in order to learn about Love.

"Yes, that's it."

What?

"I think we both fell for Love."

But you must have fallen before me. Before we knew each other.

"Is that true?"

You mean we knew each other before?

"Perhaps. I loved you the moment I first felt your presence."

And I always loved you.

"You know what we need?"

No idea.

"To hit the waves. It's too much to process on land."

I'm with you.

We run to the van and change into swimwear. A handful of dried apricots and raisins, a swig of water and we're ready to surf.

It's like meeting an old friend. The sky-blue water welcomes us with splashing arms. We make our way to the back line and scan the ocean. A rippling set arrives and we race to grab the arcing face.

The afternoon drifts lazily into a spectacular maroon-and-pink sunset. I have stowed away a small bottle of champagne in the van. The plastic flutes are in the cooler box. I grab what we need and walk back to Lailah.

It takes only a minute to fling open the blanket and pour the drinks.

"May I make a toast?"

Of course.

"To falling for Love."

Falling for Love.

I am not sure what that means but it has a nice ring to it.

Neither of us feels like going home so we find a local restaurant, enjoy a candlelit dinner and then collapse on the bed. I open the sunroof and we stare at the sparkling heavens.

I guess we come from somewhere out there.

Nothing but stillness. I watch Lailah slowly breathing in the starlight. She is already fast asleep.

* * *

One evening Lailah walks in the door. "Gosh, when did everything become work, work, work?"

I give her a kiss. *Hey sweetheart. Stressful day?*

"Running this organisation is quite demanding. How did your meeting go?"

All good. Would you like me to massage your shoulders?

"I need a hot bath, lavender oil, candles ..."

Consider it done.

"Can we get away this weekend?"

Sure. What do you have in mind?

"The north shore. Music. Good food."

Great waves and chilling together.

"Yes. Plenty of us-time."

I grab her and tickle her sides. She screeches with laughter and kicks wildly.

You know the word to make it stop ...

"Tickl ... tickle ... tic ... ticklelitus!"

What took you so long?

"Do you know how hard it is to say 'ticklelitus' when you are being tickled?"

I smile and kiss her passionately. We fall into a delicious frenzy of soft bites and luscious licks ... gradually succumbing to the exquisite ache in our bodies ... surrendering to the divine ebb and flow ...

It's the end of the week. Everything is packed. My foot presses the accelerator and we are on the road to the north shore. Fleetwood Mac's Go Your Own Way is echoing through the van. Soon it switches to the Cold Fact album by Sixto Rodriguez.

"Your music ... it's like being stuck in a time warp."

I love Rodriguez. Legendary anarchist-poet-warrior.

"Really?"

Free-thinking soul guitar.

"Ok." She rubs my leg affectionately.

We decide on Kalihiwai Point, an epic right point break located off the beaten path. It is not long before the boards are out and we are paddling into the sapphire water.

Sitting on the back line, I glance over at Lailah. My heart feels so full. This is without doubt one of the happiest days of my life. We are very fortunate – soul mates, best friends and lovers. Being with her is the deepest joy I can imagine.

We flow through the day in our usual relaxed fashion, interspersing serene surfing and refreshing ocean spray with soporific ambles along the beach. Later we sprawl on our blanket and gently stroke each other's backs, giggling contentedly in the soft breeze.

Life seems perfect.

We have dinner at a lovely seafood restaurant. The walls are adorned with paintings depicting expansive ocean vistas, cocooning us in magnificent streaks of blues and greens. I move the flickering candle to one side and place my hand upon Lailah's.

Are we going to plan our wedding soon?

Her face lights up. "Thought you'd never ask."

Your girlfriends would probably like to be involved.

"Absolutely."

Do you have any dates in mind?

"You revealed yourself to me in February."

Shall we set the date for February 7?

"Yes please."

I shake her hand. *Done. I can't wait.*

Lailah immediately whips out her phone and begins texting her friends.

"I'm so excited!"

After dinner we drive to the parking area of Secret Beach then clamber onto our soft bed. Lying on my pillow, I gaze into her beautiful eyes.

I love you so much.

"I love you with all my heart."

We cuddle closely and tenderly as the sweet night gradually overtakes us.

* * *

In the morning I wake alone. I am immediately unsettled.

The note stuck to the window reads: 'So happy and peaceful. Went for a morning walk.'

A terrible feeling of anxiety. I try to get a grip. What's the matter with me?

Locate the guidebook on the front seat. 'Kauapea Beach, known mostly by its nickname Secret Beach, is a 914-metre long beach located between Kalihiwai Bay and Kilauea Point. It is accessed by a steep trail which is not marked. The beach offers privacy, space and lush scenery but the ocean tends to be rough and is subject to extremely strong currents, especially in the winter. Proceed with caution: Walking on the lava rocks to the left of Secret Beach is only safe on the calmest summer days and when the surf report announces small waves less than half a metre high. Remember, Kauai has the highest drowning rate of all the Hawaiian Islands.'

Discard it, find my clothes, start the hike down to Secret Beach. Notice the many warning signs along the way: 'use the buddy system' … 'when in doubt, don't go out' … 'keep off the rocks'. Heart beating in my chest.

I scan the shoreline. *Lailah! Lailah!*

Where is she?

A woman is shouting hysterically in the distance. I sprint over to her.

What happened? What's going on?

"My son! My son!"

I shake her shoulders. *Tell me!*

"He was swept off the rocks and a woman jumped in after him."

Dizzy. Sick feeling in my stomach.

What did she look like?

"Blonde curls, slim –"

How long ago?

"About 15 minutes."

Have you called the Coast Guard?

"Yes, yes."

Waves are pounding the rocks. Impossible to get a closer look. Run to the sandy beach. Cup my hands. *Lailah! Lailah!*

Rescue crew arrives from the Kauai Fire Department. Helicopter commences an aerial search. Blanket around shoulders. Dazed ... nauseous. Lifeguards patrolling the shoreline. The agony of waiting.

Official stride, ominous. The mother's face crumples. Screaming against the facts. Approaching me. Please no, don't say it. They found her body. Needles piercing my back and shoulders. Eyes exploding into tears. Everything caves in. Blackness.

Light green walls ... white bedding ... intravenous drip ...

Where am I?

"Wilcox Memorial Hospital. You had a terrible shock."

Lailah!

Tears flow down my cheeks. No. No. No.

Discharged after a couple of days, I collect the van and drive home.

Walking in the door to utter desolation. The searing emptiness. The sun has disappeared. Everything is grey and bleak.

Notify our organisation and her friends. Cards arrive. Phone rings. Staring into the fridge. Staring at the dark television. Staring out the window.

The funeral is arranged. Suited and booted. Deliver a brief eulogy. Lost in a dream of activities. Collapse on the sofa. Pizza and beer. Living in my dressing gown. Who is that man in the mirror?

Shave after a month. Take the surfboard to Kealia. Spend all day crying on the beach, lost in the anguish, everything a reminder of us.

The absolute devastation. Nothing will bring her back to me.

After six months I return to work but my heart is not in it. I surrender the reins to our most experienced manager. Everyone insists that I need to keep busy, that I shouldn't leave. I cannot bear to stay.

Rattling through the house like an unseen ghost. Watching old movies. Going for short walks in the park. Miserable and alone. Perhaps I should have made friends.

A year goes by. The sharp pain settles into a dull ache. I miss her constantly.

Relentlessly despondent, I am traipsing along Kealia beach. It's been ages since I breathed this wonderful air. After a while I unfurl the old blanket and gaze out across the ocean.

In the corner of my eye, a green-silver-gold glimmer. Suddenly it's hovering before me.

You dare show your face here?

Came to deliver a message.

What is it?

Lailah is living in your home world.

She was also a fallen angel?

Indeed.

Why did she die?

You know the answer.

For Love.

Your new Guardian arrives soon.

Whoop-di-do.

Then it is gone, leaving me with minimal consolation and relief.

I stand up, remove my shirt and go for a long swim. Perhaps the warm ocean will rinse away some of the heartache.

* * *

Our wedding date is fast approaching. It's unbearable. I want to run away and be swallowed whole by the earth.

Where would we have been married? In Kauai or Oahu? On the beach? What kind of dress? A big event or something more intimate? These questions plague me.

In the end I decide to face it head on. Two days before, I drive to the north shore and check into a hotel near Hanalei Bay, a place that holds many sweet memories of our time together. The concierge organises a private table on the beach, with two place settings, flowers, champagne and our own waiter.

It is February 7. I take a quiet walk along the shoreline. Sitting on a wooden bench I slowly page through our album, tracing my fingers along the poignant photographs. Finally I utter a soft prayer.

I miss you so much, my sweetheart.

A pleasant shiver along my spine then a gentle peace. Probably a Messenger. I close my eyes to sense the energy. It's so familiar …

"I miss you too, my darling."

Lailah? Is that you?

"You know I cannot reveal myself. I have permission only to say a few words."

I love you!

"I love you too."

Tears are rolling down my cheeks.

What are you doing here?

"I'm your new Guardian."

Wow. That was unexpected.

"It is the only way I can stay close to you."

I'll take anything on offer.

"Thought as much."

Where have you been for a year?

"I was assigned to an Overseer. A kind of apprenticeship."

You going to get promoted?

"I don't know the plan."

I smile. *Above your grade?*

"Probably. You going somewhere?"

Don't you know what day it is?

"February 7?"

Our wedding day. Care to join me?

"It will be my honour."

With our energy fields touching it feels like we are holding hands. I wipe my eyes and compose myself as we proceed to our celebratory dinner.

The waiter has been briefed about my situation and maintains an air of respect and solemnity. I cannot talk to Lailah while he is serving us but I know she is sitting beside me. I am certain she is adoring the flowers, candles and expansive pink sunset, so reminiscent of our romantic engagement party.

I raise my glass for our customary toast.

To everlasting love.

"Everlasting love," I hear her whisper back.

My heart feels warm and full.

Later we make our way to the plush hotel room. She ensconces me in her beautiful energy and I sleep deeply and restfully for the first time in months. I don't even remember dreaming.

* * *

Today is a new day. I wake with a vitality coursing through my spirit. Lailah is here; I can sense her. It makes my world cheerful.

I am sitting on the edge of the bed wondering about this life. How is it that you never quite have everything you want? Perhaps you are fortunate enough to have a good income but you struggle to find the right love. You have a great relationship but your health fails. You love someone with all your heart and they leave you.

Here I am with the love of my life. I cannot see or touch her. We cannot interact.

I sigh deeply and stare out the window.

The phone rings. It's the concierge checking on last night's event. After expressing my gratitude he asks what I plan to do for the rest of the day. He recommends an air tour of the magnificent Napali Coast: 27 kilometres of stunning coastline lined with immense cliffs, lush green valleys and cascading waterfalls. It seems like a fitting way to end the north shore commemoration.

After the breathtaking excursion I check out of the hotel, relish a quick lunch and drive south. I am at peace. All I want now is to go home.

The next few days are filled with thinking and planning. With Lailah beside me I revert to right-mindedness. It's time to get back to work. Time to contribute to society.

I pull out a recent organisation report. The statistics are frightening: 12% of the world's population are living without clean drinking water; 40% don't have access to adequate sanitation; and 2,000 children die every day from diarrhoea. It is essential to provide WASH to the poorest people – water, sanitation, hygiene.

Running an organisation really doesn't suit my temperament. I don't care for the constant meetings and administration. Instead of returning to manage our charitable company, I determine to visit Africa and apply myself directly. I will continue to work with my company, utilising their social and business connections and providing useful on-location reporting.

With Lailah physically gone there is nothing holding me back. I sell the house within a month and buy a small apartment in Kauai which provides a secure base. I furnish it with significant mementos of our relationship then give a key to a neighbour for safe-keeping.

All her clothing and excess possessions are delivered to a charity shop. Finally, after saying a little prayer, I sell her pearls. The money will be used to create Lailah's legacy, leaving a reminder of her beautiful spirit on the planet.

My charitable organisation works out a general itinerary and purchases the aeroplane tickets. There will be no hotels or fancy living for me. I aim to immerse myself in the local communities, experience their struggles and find practical ways to resolve their challenges. I will be recording all my adventures and uploading as a video log onto the company website. Hopefully this will encourage marketing and fundraising efforts.

I am relaxing on the plane and marvelling at the recent life changes. It's interesting how quickly things move once you create a clear vision. Vision, intention and commitment seem to be crucial keys for shifting reality.

And so begins my tour of Compassion and Service.

First stop, Mozambique. The local guide introduces me to a tiny and very dangerous predator – the mosquito. Although malaria was eradicated in Western countries more than 60 years ago, in many African countries it is still destroying families and communities. The solution is very simple: insecticide-treated bed nets.

This immediately becomes a fanatical endeavour. I upload a couple of videos reflecting the personal and commercial mayhem caused by malaria and plead for a huge donation of nets. With the right marketing tweaks, the videos go viral. Thousands of nets start arriving. The impact on the communities is enormous.

Two months later I fly north to Uganda. We continue with the mosquito net programme. It feels easier to ask for life-saving products than money, so I upload another video highlighting the water issues and requesting water purification tablets. Soon we have an abundance. Distribution is left in the hands of the village elders.

Across the border is South Sudan, a region devastated by intense conflict. Many villages are without basic sanitation facilities such as basins and toilets, making it easy for disease to spread. Another video educates about their plight and appeals for simple washing facilities. Senegal faces similar issues. Fixing village water sources becomes as important as the battle against malaria.

I am sitting on a beach in Senegal, staring out over the Atlantic Ocean. A cool breeze is blowing. Numerous thoughts are blazing through my mind. It is incredible that millions of people across the world are living in abject poverty under abhorrent circumstances. Yet television networks broadcast self-indulgent reality shows that invite us to watch the antics of the rich and famous.

Is it really more important to gape at a ten-thousand-dollar party for a celebrity's dog? Imagine how many mosquito nets that money could buy. What happened to social responsibility? Why are we celebrating fame, physical appearance and wealth when the world is burning?

I will not rest until every drop of sweat has flowed and every cent has been spent for the alleviation of suffering. These are our fellow human beings – brothers and sisters in every country.

Travelling west across the continent, I visit Ethiopia and discover how farm animals can help families immensely. Chickens and goats provide eggs, milk and cheese and a steady source of income. I quickly upload another video onto the website.

Three months later I am informed that our videos have become an internet sensation, drawing millions of viewers and lots of media attention. We link with experienced charitable organisations like World Vision and WaterAid and spread the word. World Vision also has a brilliant website called Must Have Gifts – it takes only a few clicks to despatch nets, water purification tablets and other life-saving products to struggling communities.

These humanitarian projects have created a wonderful sense of fulfilment in me. I remember Lailah once saying that altruism is one of the greatest sources of happiness. It has certainly helped me transcend sadness and grief.

A long year has come to an end. I need to fly home for a short break and to strategise the next programme. As the aeroplane door closes I notice a range of feelings ... triumph ... joy ... heartache. This job is far from finished.

* * *

Back home the apartment feels cold and lifeless. There are no memories here, only stark reminders of what we shared. I have this awful sense of not belonging.

After a few days I load the van and head south to Poipu Beach. Perhaps a few hours in the ocean will help me settle. On the radio a piece of African music is playing. Strangely, it makes me feel better.

It is fairly quiet when I arrive. The sun is low on the horizon and the waves are pumping. Perfect conditions. I grab the board and run into the water.

Oh, that familiar feeling! Paddling into the swell, duck-diving incoming waves, waiting at the back line ... then the exhilaration of catching the face and carving through ocean spray. I shout at the top of my lungs and my voice reverberates in the curling wave. Awesome!

Time disappears amid the serene surfing.

After a lunch of sweet breads and fruit salad, I stretch out on the blanket and stare into the hazy afternoon sky. There's that shiver of energy. Lailah!

Hey ...

No response.

Wish you were laying here with me ...

Usual silence.

I sigh heavily. This is my life. Empty and solitary.

There is a sudden buzzing around my ear. It's the hummingbird.

My brow creases. *What do you want?*

Your anger only hurts you.

Yeah? Where's my choice in the matter? I didn't ask to be alone.

People move on. We are all catching waves.

I prefer to surf with my partner.

You could love another.

Lailah is the one for me.

I look it straight in the eye. I will wait for her forever.

There is a being in your home world called Octavio Paz. He ascended in 1998. He said: 'The art of love – is it the art of dying? To love is to die and live again and die again: it is liveliness.'

My hands move to cover my face. Tears sting my eyes and stream down my cheeks.

No idea what that means.

In time.

I am sobbing heavily. My chest is heaving. Lailah, I miss you!

It's like screaming into deep space. No one seems to hear.

I stare at the rolling ocean for another hour. Peace and clarity course into my energy. There is nothing here for me anymore. I unpack the contents of the van, pile it on the beach and tape a note to one of the boards: 'Take what you want. It's free'.

I need to catch my own wave. It's time to return to Africa.

* * *

The van goes to one of Lailah's friends. I debate about the apartment but decide to keep it. It may be devoid of memories but it's a haven for our mementos. I can't let it go.

A few meetings and a fair amount of planning and I am ready to depart. Tickets in hand, I head to the airport. For a moment an anomalous thought enters my mind: I'm going home.

Phew, it's hot! And dusty. My guide meets me and we get straight to work. 13 million people in the Horn of Africa are threatened by starvation. Kenya, Ethiopia, Somalia and Tanzania are experiencing the worst drought in 60 years. There is a severe food crisis.

I wonder if a Westerner can conceive of such a slow and painful death. With our sugary diets and overflowing supermarkets, starvation is probably the last thing on our minds. It's an excruciating and unnecessary way to leave this world.

We work tirelessly to provide emergency food, clean water, agricultural support and healthcare. Education seems like a privilege instead of a fundamental right. Being on the bottom rung of the planetary ladder removes a lot of choices. Capitalist and religious ideologies become ludicrous: What use are the phrases 'work hard and you can achieve anything' or 'have more faith' or 'the world is your oyster' to starving children?

They are just trying to survive.

My job vacillates between heartbreaking and thrilling. It is incredibly liberating not focusing on oneself. Every day a little part of my ego dies and I fall deeper into Love. It is wordlessly beautiful.

Six months pass. I am walking through a dusty village in Sudan. Civil war raged in this country for more than two decades, killing at least half a million people and displacing millions more. The war was suspended only a few years ago. It is now a place of extreme hunger and poverty.

Crack-crack! Crack!

I am flung a few metres and land behind a wall. Stunned, I recollect the guide's warning: 'You only hear the sound of gunfire after the bullets have traversed a long distance'. It's usually too late to do anything by the time the sound arrives. I run my fingers over my body. No wounds.

A calmness comes over me. That energy ...

Lailah, is that you?

"Run, my love. Run!"

My heart starts pounding. That building in the distance. Legs suddenly heavy, arms floundering. Everything slows ... my field of vision widens ... tears cloud my eyes ...

"Run!" she screams.

Crack-crack! Crack-crack-crack!

Dizzying sprint. Too far. Not going to make it. Wetness in my hair. Dripping on my face.

Lailah!

I am in her arms. Red spatter on my shirt. Disoriented. Blackness.

The familiar smell. Hospital. Doctor with clipboard. Friendly grin. "Ah, you're back with us."

What happened?

"Flesh wound through the scalp. Nothing serious. You'll have a scar though."

Uh, thanks.

"How are you feeling?"

Um .. ok.

"Shall I let your wife know you're awake?"

My wife?

"Mrs Walker."

I smile. *Yes please.*

In the doorway stands my radiant angel. *Lailah! It's really you.*

Then we are hugging and kissing and chatting as if we were never apart.

Where are we?

"Kenya."

How?

"We jumped."

Like I used to jump with you?

She nods seriously.

Uh oh. You have broken the rules.

"I couldn't watch you get hurt."

Been there. Done that.

"What's going to happen now?"

You know the answer.

"The Chasers will come."

Indeed.

* * *

I reach for her hand and smile. *How much time do we have?*

"Those Chasers were adept at tracking you down."

I don't remember.

"We need to jump away from this energy trail."

Suits me.

"Shall we go home?"

How about Kealia beach?

We make the leap. Wow! Did I really give up this amazing ability?

Sapphire waves are curling in the distance. I discard my shoes and let my toes scrunch contentedly in the sand. A gentle breeze ruffles my hair. I take a deep breath and sigh.

I've missed you so much.

"It's been really tough."

Come here.

I pull her close and hold her tight.

Never want to let you go.

"Me neither."

We are both crying and smiling as our heart energies reconnect.

I whisper in her ear. *So tell me, my darling, am I dating an older woman?*

She slaps my shoulder. "You don't want to know."

Really? That old?

"You should be calling me Ma'am."

Don't know if I can do this.

"Stop teasing!"

Ok, give me the juice.

"About 3000 years old."

Wow.

"Can you handle it?"

I pack up with laughter. *Of course. I love you.*

"You silly man."

We amble along the shoreline for a while. It feels good to hold hands again.

What was it like apprenticing to an Overseer?

She shakes her head. "They are sticklers for rules. Great administrators. It is a necessary job. Someone has to maintain order."

Did you have access to a higher level?

"Hmm?"

The repository of knowledge.

"Of course. Do you know that the majority of Walkers incarnate?"

Meaning?

"They are born as human babies and live a full earthly life."

No problems with birth certificates.

"Falling as an adult body is quite rare."

Either way you lose your memories.

She nods. "That's a given."

So they truly walk among us.

"Yep. Messengers, Guardians and Walkers."

They walk among us.

"Indeed."

We sit down on the sand and gaze out over the rippling ocean.

"What are we going to do? We can't start running again."

Are you allowed to fall?

"Every being has free will ..."

I notice the hesitancy in her voice.

You don't want to return?

Her eyes lock onto mine. "I came to learn about the human condition and to understand love."

And your mission has been achieved?

She stares at her feet. "You helped me achieve it. You still are."

But ...

"I am learning so much from the Overseer."

You're still apprenticing?

"We can be in many places at once."

Aren't Guardians earth-bound?

"I'm not really a Guardian. I just have special permission to watch over you."

Who gave you permission?

"The Overseer."

Aha.

"Staying here jeopardises my future."

Ouch.

"I am sorry."

This is us you're talking about.

"My love for you will never die."

Are you saying we should explore separate paths?

"I will always be yours."

Tell me.

"I don't know. Yes. Maybe."

Wow.

"Would you prefer to start running?"

I frown and ruffle my hair. A heavy stillness enfolds us.

Eventually I realise the answer. *No.*

"What does your essence tell you?"

I want to be with you. I need to continue my work in Africa.

"A similar dilemma."

This can't be happening. It's not the way it's supposed to end.

Will you wait for me?

"Always."

My heart is wrenching. I feel dizzy and nauseous.

Lailah, I can't live without you.

She grabs my hand. "Yes, you can."

Hot tears burn my cheeks. The world is spinning.

Will you still be my Guardian?

"I hope so."

We lay on the beach until sunset, both of us trying to assimilate our decision.

Finally I stand up and extend my hand. *Stay with me tonight?*

"Of course, my darling."

We jump to the apartment. She watches me shower and eat dinner. Then we clamber into bed and curl up in each other's arms.

Lailah, I love you with all my heart.

"I will never stop loving you."

It is impossible to sleep. I drowsily hold her all night. My heart relentlessly wrestles with me.

When the morning light breaks, we make the jump back to Africa.

The last image I see is her bouncing golden curls disappearing into another reality.

* * *

Love can make you crazy. I am terribly unsettled. What it really the right decision?

The only way I can cope is to plough into various charitable projects. I work all hours, travelling to different African countries, liaising with my organisation, uploading videos, begging for supplies. The publicity is producing strong financial results so we widen our campaign to include humanitarian projects in South Asia.

Occasionally I notice negative comments on our website. Detractors saying that our work is a drop in the ocean of poverty, that money is being poured into a bottomless pit. No doubt these individuals are sitting in cushy offices with secure jobs and nice homes. Once you have stared into a starving child's eyes, your heart is forever connected to the truth.

The only real question is: How can I alleviate the suffering of my fellow humans?

After nine hectic months I start to feel burnt out. Finishing up a project in Tanzania, I determine to take a recuperative break. My guide suggests the Zanzibar archipelago, located about 25 kilometres off the coast of Tanzania in the warm Indian Ocean. There are numerous small islands and two large ones, Pemba and Unguja.

Confusingly, Unguja island is informally called Zanzibar. It's other name is The Spice Island which sounds rather exotic. I spend the first two days hiking the beautiful Jozani Forest nature trails. Then I drift along the many sparkling beaches. Matemwe, Pwani Mchangani, Kiwengwa, Uroa, Bwejuu and Jambiani are situated on the east side of the island and feature brilliant white sand, shallow sandbars and dancing turquoise waters.

A short excursion to the northern tip of the island reveals the picturesque town of Nungwi, ensconced among banana palms, mangroves and coconut trees. I make my way down to the beach and dive into the undulating waves. Afterward I sit on the warm sand and marvel at the natural environment. Zanzibar is a resplendent paradise.

A familiar green-silver-gold plumage breezes past my face. The inscrutable gaze of the hummingbird settles upon me.

Greetings, Avatar.

A subtle nod. I guess the first move is mine.

Tell me about Lailah. Is she well? Is she still my Guardian?

Another barely distinguishable nod.

I sigh a little. This is going to be interesting.

Is Lailah going to become an Overseer?

A long silence. Then a sage response.

Do not concern yourself with advancement. Ponder this question: What lies beyond knowledge?

I swish my toes through the shimmering sand.

Um ... a myriad realities, endless knowledge ... ah ... the Light?

The Light is the underlying all-pervasive Source. What surrounds the Light?

Rubbing my unshaven chin. Frowning.

Uh ... Love?

Light, Love then Knowledge.

So I should pursue the Light?

You can experience glimpses of the Source; you can swim in the Light; but you will never fully return until you can harmonise with and move through the energy of Love.

Ah, yes, I remember your words.

I sit quietly and watch the sky-blue ocean.

So it's all about surrendering into Love.

Indeed.

And acting with Love.

Lao Tzu, author of the Tao Te Ching, ascended in 531 BC. He taught: 'The highest virtue is to act without a sense of self. The highest kindness is to give without condition.'

It seems all the great teachers reside in my world.

I clasp my hands behind my head, lay back and stare at the heavens.

Nothing to chase, nothing to do, nothing to seek. Only Love.

Jalal ad-Din Rumi ascended in 1273. He said: 'And when you are the Lover at last, you don't care. Whatever you know or don't – only Love is real.'

The wings flitter wildly. A blur of colour. The hummingbird disappears.

An hour passes as I meditate upon the divine wisdom. Then I walk to a restaurant and enjoy a sunset dinner.

At the end of the week I pack my bag and return to the dusty villages and big cities of Africa. There is much work to do. And much loving-kindness to give.

I immerse myself in various humanitarian projects. I am still linked to my organisation and together we organise an enormous multi-country charity drive. My videos continue to garner worldwide interest and valuable media attention. Money and supplies pour into our health and education programmes.

Over the next four years we manage to spread vast amounts of love and joy. It is without doubt the most fulfilling and rewarding period of my life. I have spent every cent of my own money, distributed Lailah's legacy and even sold the apartment in Kauai.

I am a man of the people. Together we live on a wing and a prayer.

As for my sweetheart, I think of her often but have learned to live without her. It's been a steady and painful transition. My heart aches occasionally. I hope we will be reunited one day.

I am wrapping up a project in South Sudan. It is dusk. I am following the path back to the main village. Descending a hill, I notice a commotion beneath the trees. I hurry over to investigate and stumble across two gunmen training AK47 rifles on a group of small children.

What's going on here?

"Stay out of it, Westerner. This does not concern you."

What do you want with these children?

"I'm warning you. Leave now."

Absolutely not.

I position myself between the rifles and the children and glare assertively at the guerrillas. The weapons are lowered but the belligerent expressions remain.

Turning around, I command loudly: *Run to your mothers, children! Now!*

Little feet scatter in all directions. A slow moment passes.

Crack-crack! is the last sound I hear.

* * *

The shearing of my consciousness. Innumerable images flashing through my mind. Lailah has fallen off the boat. The reveal – she knows! A church in Iceland. Broken the rules. Red-eyed Chasers. Beautiful islands. Such deep love! Tears streaming down my face. An interlude in my world. The thrill of Hawaii. A new life. Surfing those gorgeous waves. The engagement on the beach. Lailah is gone! The overwhelming grief. My work in Africa. A fleeting reunion. More grief. Resolute devoted charitable work.

I know who I am! A being with no name and no gender. A sparkling ball of pure energy, a shimmering translucent mist.

An outstretched hand appears. *I am the Messenger sent to welcome you.*

Everything is so still and peaceful. I have missed this place very much.

I was known as Rabindranath Tagore. I ascended in 1941.

My energy seems different. It is fluttering and streaming into pure white.

What's happening to me?

Soft laughter. *I once wrote: 'What is this light that dances at the centre of my life? This flood of joy must indeed be love, for love is the only reality and it is not a mere sentiment. It is the truth that lies at the heart of all creation.'*

Do all great teachers speak in mysteries?

You don't recognise yourself?

Is this Love?

Of course.

Why am I getting brighter?

You are adjusting to the emanation of your evolved essence.

What?

Come with me.

We float along meandering pathways bordered by immense statues and majestic fountains. Flowers of every colour sway among solemn trees in resplendent gardens. The sweetest notes of ethereal music dance across the marble steps. The Sacred Temple!

What are we doing here?

I cannot accompany you further.

The white-yellow being turns away from me, as if in pain.

What is it?

I am no longer able to look upon you.

I focus my awareness on my essence. It is radiating brightly, like an intensely shining star.

You have become a 'burning one'. They are waiting for you.

No one may enter the temple. Yet I know this is my true home; it is where I belong.

The colossal doors swing open. I walk into a huge room, the walls adorned with opulent paintings and intricate weavings. A few represent earth's major religions, others contain strange and beautiful fractal images with meanings I cannot ascertain. A levitating map of the universe hangs in one corner. I peruse it for a while.

Far in the distance is a stone archway. The calligraphic etching declares the Hall of Knowledge. I flow toward it and discover a boundless library containing books in multifarious languages. In the centre of the hall a large luminous book lies open on a carved antique desk. It seems to operate by intention: The moment I think of a question, it activates an immersive holographic answer.

I spend time watching the life of Lailah. Her heartaches, trials and tribulations. The grief she endured because of the choice we made. Her deep love for me. The recent graduation ceremony that conferred the title of Overseer upon her. There are only seven Overseers and she is now one of them. I notice that her essence has changed into radiant white streaked with mauve. She is content.

I wonder how I came to be here. Immediately I am shown the transformative power of Love. The life I lived, the choices I made. The vacancy created when a Keeper moved to an even higher plane of existence. My inevitable destination. Spiritual gravity dictates that a being's essence always draws the being to where it belongs. As one evolves and the energy signature transmutes, the environment needs to change too. It's about the resonance of energies.

Here I am.

A passage from Jonathan Livingston Seagull, the book by Richard Bach, leaps into my mind: 'So this is heaven, he thought, and he had to smile at himself. It was hardly respectful to analyse heaven in the very moment that one flies up to enter it.'

I laugh softly. Joy fills my being.

The final doorway presents an enormous chamber. Extravagant carvings decorate the expansive stone walls. Twelve shimmering obelisks stand guard in a wide circle. Purple robes flutter in an invisible breeze. Eleven illuminated beings surround the dazzling stream of Light. Smiling, they beckon me to take my place as the twelfth Keeper.

It is beyond surreal. The longer I gaze into the Light the more I realise the hilarity of the multitudinous illusions. None of it matters. The stories seem so real when you are living them. What were the words of the hummingbird? Ah, yes: 'Life is a series of stories that you create in order to learn about Love. Your job is to immerse yourself in each story but not attach to it.'

Life is not about the self and the ego. It is not about the accumulation of wealth and power. It is not about deceit, manipulation, abuse or harm. It is not about ignoring the suffering of fellow beings. It is not about the rightness and righteousness of our many stories.

Life is the journey through the energy of Love.

We send Messengers and Guardians to innumerable dimensions. Walkers incarnate and fall onto countless worlds. They walk among you, forever whispering love to your essence. The rest is in your hands. Your journey and destination are the result of the choices you make. You are creating your own reality.

I take a break from the Light and walk to an alcove window. The endless landscape stretches before me: a spectacular consortium of dancing flowers, majestic trees, stone pathways, imposing statues and grand fountains. Sparkling translucent mists converse serenely with ascended beings near the lotus pond.

A blurring flicker of wings. The familiar green-silver-gold plumage. Deep stillness immediately settles upon me.

Greetings, Avatar.

Here you are.

Here I am.

Was it really worth fighting for, being brave for, risking everything for?

You mean Love?

The usual quietness.

Absolutely. For Love in all its forms.

It stares at me with that inscrutable gaze.

The energy surrounding the Source is Love.

The Keepers of the Light encircle the Source.

Therefore the Keepers of the Light are Love.

Ah. The Hall of Knowledge. The Keepers. The Light.

I am the Lover at last. Whatever I know or don't – only Love is real.

In the end there is only Love and Light.

The hummingbird rests on the window ledge and the incessant motion ceases.

You're rather small for a mover and shaker of worlds.

Who knows where you'll be one day.

Indeed.

I could swear I see the faintest smile. The eyes glint then it flits across and disappears into the dazzling stream of Light.

There is a catalyst in the system. Avatar of the Light.

I throw my head back and laugh.

That darn hummingbird!

Stephen Shaw's Books

Visit the website: www.i-am-stephen-shaw.com

I Am contains spiritual and mystical teachings from enlightened masters that point the way to love, peace, bliss, freedom and spiritual awakening.

Heart Song takes you on a mystical adventure into creating your reality and manifesting your dreams, and reveals the secrets to attaining a fulfilled and joyful life.

They Walk Among Us is a love story spanning two realities. Explore the mystery of the angels. Discover the secrets of Love Whispering.

The Other Side explores the most fundamental question in each reality. What happens when the physical body dies? Where do you go? Expand your awareness. Journey deep into the Mystery.

Reflections offers mystical words for guidance, meditation and contemplation. Open the book anywhere and unwrap your daily inspiration.

5D is the Fifth Dimension. Discover ethereal doorways hidden in the fabric of space-time. Seek the advanced mystical teachings.

Star Child offers an exciting glimpse into the future on earth. The return of the gods and the advanced mystical teachings. And the ultimate battle of light versus darkness.

The Tribe expounds the joyful creation of new Earth. What happened after the legendary battle of Machu Picchu? What is Christ consciousness? What is Ecstatic Tantra?

The Fractal Key reveals the secrets of the shamans. This handbook for psychonauts discloses the techniques and practices used in psychedelic healing and transcendent journeys.

CPSIA information can be obtained
at www.ICGtesting.com
Printed in the USA
BVOW06s1754050117
472579BV00009BA/131/P